Welcome
TO THE
FIFTH ESTATE

Nancy!
Glad we've gotten
to be friends over the
past year. Best wishes

Welcome
TO THE
FIFTH ESTATE

How to Create and Sustain a
Winning Social Media Strategy

GEOFF LIVINGSTON

Introduction by Adam Ostrow

Bartleby Press
Washington • Baltimore

Bartleby Press

8600 Foundry Street
Savage Mill Box 2043
Savage, MD 20763
800-953-9929
www.BartlebythePublisher.com

ISBN: 978-0910155-86-1
Library of Congress Control Number: 2011929516

Printed in the United States of America

To my daughter, Soleil Maya Livingston,
born on October 29, 2010

Contents

Acknowledgements

As always a special hat tip to my publisher, Jeremy Kay. Thank you for believing in me. Thank you Jennifer Goode Stevens, Bill Sledzik and Tom Livingston (yes, Dad) for editing.

My business partner Kami Huyse, who drafted the chapter on measurement, deserves special gratitude. When in doubt, trust a subject matter expert! Adam Ostrow also made an invaluable contribution in writing the excellent introduction to *Welcome to the Fifth Estate*!

Ike Pigott is a great friend and actually named the book after reading some draft material on my blog. What better way to celebrate the Fifth Estate then to heed its commentary—and reward it.

My beautiful wife, Caitlin Livingston, was 4-9 months

pregnant during the writing of this book. She, too, believed in me, and wouldn't let me quit, even when I hit a wall.

Finally, I am indebted to you, all of my friends, fans and followers who support me online. This book would not be possible without you. I hope you enjoy it.

Introduction

by Adam Ostrow

By the end of 2009, fifty-eight percent of Americans were watching TV and using the Internet simultaneously. Among those that were doing so, the average consumer was spending 3 hours and 30 minutes each month engaged with both mediums at the same time.[1] While that's one quantitative way to look at an obvious trend in shifting media consumption habits that many have observed anecdotally for some time, here's another: At some point within the next decade, there will be between 15-50 billion devices on our planet that are in some way connected to the Internet.[2]

At the time of this writing, that trend is probably showing itself most visibly in the living room with smartphones and

1

tablets, or at the local cafe or in the car with the increasingly distracted people in our lives firing away texts and e-mails instead of focusing on (gasp!) real world conversation.

But the trend is only at the beginning. The innovations we've seen in the last few years—from the rise of social media, to the increasing ubiquity of smartphones, to advances in wireless bandwidth—have set the stage for dramatic changes to take place in our culture, our media and the role of the corporation.

With everything from cars to kitchens about to get connected to the Internet, a new way of thinking is required.

The Like Economy

It took the Facebook "like" button just 8 months to find itself embedded on more than 2 million websites and applications.[3] While on one hand that helps solidify Facebook as the most dominant social network by a significant margin—and builds it a much bigger moat than leading networks before it— on the other it creates an important new reality for businesses.

There's a battle for mindshare on Facebook, and much of it is now being fought on content and e-commerce sites, where "likes" equate to links in user's news feeds that create exposure for brands. Similarly, within the walls of Facebook, "likes" equate to popularity for the pages of businesses large and small. Already, we're seeing this data applied to what to-date has been the largest source of traffic for most businesses: search. In October, 2010, Facebook and Microsoft rolled out an integration of "Likes" within Bing's search results that gives preference to links that have been "liked" by your friends.

"Likes" are starting to show up in other areas too. A

number of startups are allowing users to "check in" to television shows from their smartphones and tablets, and share their viewing experience with friends. One of those services —Clicker—scored a partnership with Facebook that allows them to make recommendations for what to watch, based both on your own viewing and "liking" history, as well as data gleaned from your friend's activities and conversations on the social network.

The growing ubiquity of location services like Foursquare (and Facebook, with its Places product) has similar implications to the "like" button. As of this writing, Foursquare is said to be working on a recommendation engine that suggests venues based on your prior check-ins and places that your friends like.

Every Company Needs a Content Strategy

The new realities of the "like" economy have only further increased the pressure on corporations to become content producers and gain mindshare within the social media ecosystem. While several years ago this meant blogs – or at least gaining influence with bloggers – today it means reaching consumers in their medium of choice (and choices are abound) with compelling content of your own. That's why you see not just media companies like The Wall Street Journal and MTV embracing a service like Foursquare, but also retail brands like Gap and Radio Shack. It is why you see the already clichéd Old Spice campaign being emulated (albeit with considerably less success) by companies like Cisco. And it's why you see TV networks experimenting with entertainment "check-in" services and offering prizes for watching content and broadcasting about it, even though business models are still nascent to non-existent in the space. That said, the proliferation of media and entertainment options has created a whole new set of challenges. Organizations need to be structured such that it doesn't take seven levels of approvals to post a tweet (a reality at a multi-billion dollar corporation I won't name here). Social media policies need to be crafted to keep employees nimble yet on message, but still not bigger than the brand they represent. And "influencer" needs to be redefined, looking within each medium—and within individual segments of that medium—to identify the most important people to reach.

Advertising's Evolving Role

Some might think that advertising has no place in this environment, with everything from the 30 second TV spot to the banner ad being displaced by so-called earned media. In reality, the opposite is true. Because of the wealth of data and personalization options being developed, along with increased connectivity and a digital identity that follows us across platforms and devices, unprecedented opportunities for precision messaging will emerge for marketers.

Early examples are abound. Twitter's business model went from punchline to promising in a matter of months, with "promoted tweets" showing us what a cost per engagement (a retweet, a reply, or a click) model of advertising might look like. Facebook has demonstrated the power of friend's suggestions, with ads accompanied by "likes," as well as moved into payments and the lucrative world of virtual goods that many brands are now clamoring to get inside of. On the mobile front, GPS-equipped smartphones are enabling unprecedented location targeting options in advertising, helping fuel one of the quickest creations of wealth in history with the ascent of Groupon.

It goes much further, however. With TV and radio (through advances in wireless technology) becoming Internet connected, visual and audio advertising will move from a purely push model to both push and pull. For example, that means ads on television that behave more like ads on the web, with interactivity that lets you download content, make a purchase or share something with a friend. On radio, it means being able to sync your music or talk shows from your car to your mobile to your desktop, with advertising made much more precise based on your location and listening habits.

The Fifth Estate

What's implied in all of this is that in the years to come, the multitude of choices for content and entertainment consumption will only continue to increase. Much like the advent of blogs and social media turned the print publishing world upside down in the first decade of this century, Internet connected television and radio will provide consumers with virtually unlimited options in the second and create hundreds if not thousands of new media outlets.

What's so interesting about this shift is that much of the groundwork has already been laid and much of what's to come is simply an extension of what's already been built. As consumers, we already have social profiles – in the next few years, they will simply become intertwined in more places, providing more intelligence to the devices that get us through our daily lives. As businesses, many of us are already producing content —in the next few years, we'll simply be producing more of it and providing our audiences with more ways to consume it. As non-profits and other cause-based organizations, technology has finally enabled the type of outreach we've long suspected is most impactful: local and in real-time.

The Fifth Estate presents a framework for all constituents attempting to navigate this world. Through research, case studies and a multitude of expert opinions, it presents a thoughtful look at the evolving media landscape, with lessons that will undoubtedly permeate as the next decade of change takes hold.

Chapter 1
The Rise of Citizen Media

In life there are few moments of clarity when you realize that things have completely changed, and that nothing will be the same. These moments vary in cause and significance, from the birth of a child or the assassination of president to an executive departing unexpectedly or a new technology like an iPad arriving in your home.

I described one such seminal moment in my first book *Now is Gone*. In November 2006, Jim Webb won the Virginia race for U.S. Senate. He had done the impossible–defeating George Allen, a formidable incumbent who only three months earlier was considered a serious 2008 presidential candidate for the GOP. George Allen was considered so safe for re-election that his initial campaign manager left to work on a race that was considered tougher.[4] But he was brought down by bloggers.

Allen had the misfortune of using a word, "macaca" at a

campaign event and having it caught on video. The perception began to grow that he had uttered a racial slur. The Webb campaign intentionally spread the video and talked it up through social media outlets such as blogs and YouTube. The ensuing uproar in the media and back into the blogosphere turned a runaway race into a dogfight; ultimately it cost the Republicans control of the Senate.[5]

At that moment, I knew the face of communications had been altered forever; the traditional media—the so-called watchdog "Fourth Estate"—had failed to report the story. Instead the public spread the story using social web properties until the cacophony of voices had risen to the point that the traditional media had no choice but to report on it. As a professional communicator of 13 years at the time, this moment caused me to rethink my entire approach to public relations and marketing. What had been mostly fun and experimental became the primary thrust of my business. I was launched, unexpectedly, into an incredible new career trajectory.

As evidenced by the Webb election, social media–blogs, social networks, localized-search-enabled maps, SEO, user-generated video and audio, arose with millions upon millions of content producers. These content creators and readers suddenly had achieved a new level of power and weight. More recently, turmoil in the Middle East showed that the way countries were run could change with one major initiative.

It was time to stop experimenting with new media and instead get to know everything possible about its workings. The social media boom was different than the dot-com era–users fueled the new media, not venture capital-backed startups. It became a society-fueled trend that continues to grow in scope, scale and impact. Communications has evolved more in the past ten years than it did in the previous 50, when television broadcasting took the world by storm.

Welcome to the Fifth Estate

Five years after the Webb moment, social media users have become a force of their own, community members with a voice not supplanting the media, but augmenting it. Since I wrote *Now Is Gone*, when it was called "new media," social media has assumed its place in the larger media mix. It has become the Fifth Estate.

The Fourth Estate, or the traditional media, got its nickname by policing the governments of France and Great Britain in the late 18th and early 19th centuries.[6] The French Estates General consisted of The First Estate of 300 clergy, the Second Estate of 300 nobles and the Third Estate of 600 commoners. The media fulfilled a new role, providing their readership with more factual information about political events. As a result, politicians were held to a new level of accountability. Media became the fact provider, the great source of objective information. When the politicians stepped out of line, the masses were informed. Protests, and in some cases mobs and revolution, ensued.[7]

Since the 18th century, the Fourth Estate has grown to include broadcast media forms, as well. In modern times, the Fourth Estate's role has extended into new facets of life, from business reporting (for example, the Hewlett-Packard Board scandal during Carly Fiorina's leadership) to entertainment (Lindsay Lohan's ongoing woes with the law). Perhaps the greatest moment of the Fourth Estate was the epic Watergate scandal, in which two *Washington Post* reporters—Bob Woodward and Carl Bernstein—exposed the connection between the White House and a break-in at the Democratic National Committee's offices during the 1972 U.S. presidential election. The ensuing scandal eventually caused President Richard M. Nixon to resign.

Yet, the media creates their own fallacies. PR execs swarm the traditional media (and now bloggers) to place stories. Corporations, nonprofits and politicians alike employ spinners to ensure favorable coverage, and decreasing budgets have brought about newsrooms with fewer and younger journalists[8]. While some still are authoritative, the media no longer enjoys widespread trust. According to Edelman's 2010 Trust Barometer report, most forms of traditional media are trusted by only 30-plus percent of the population.[9]

The Fifth Estate—citizen media—often introduces previously unreported, yet relevant, news, and it questions stated facts. Marshall University Professor Stephen D. Cooper proposed the concept of a Fifth Estate in his 2006 book, *Watching the Watchdog: Bloggers as the Fifth Estate*.[10] Cooper observed that blogs create a new level of accountability caused by the emergence of a Fifth Estate in our social system: The social media content creators and users keep the Fourth Estate honest. Indeed, in some cases traditional media outlets have embraced social media voices, using them to augment their own research. Consider how CNN has moved away from just presenting its own news reports and Associated Press coverage, and it now uses user-generated iReports to enrich its online offering.

The popularity of social networks, where content and

ideas can create "viral" explosions of widespread ideas. With just the right spark, increasingly accessible historical data has made it easier than ever for the media and rival campaigns to spot the mistakes and exaggerations of politicians. The Republican National Committee employees people to analyze each presidential speech for inaccuracies and then tweets them publicly. And the phenomenon is not isolated to politics. *The Washington Post* published a piece on how fan-generated media is driving sports stories.[11] Here's a snippet:

"But in the arena of sports, the arbiter of what matters is increasingly shifting from the mainstream media to the freewheeling realm of the blogosphere, where impassioned fans opine about the playing field's heroes, villains and controversies of the day."

Like the Fourth Estate, the role of the Fifth Estate has extended beyond politics to larger issues. Consider bestselling business author Charlene Li's influential role in raising the flag on Facebook's privacy-threatening advertising platform Beacon in 2007. By blogging about the questionable privacy invasions created by Beacon, she set off a tidal wave of mainstream press and blog coverage about Facebook's new advertising platform. In 2009, Iranian social media users raised the visibility of their rebellion against a rigged election to a global level. Twitter users adopted symbolic green-hued or green-emblazoned avatars to demonstrate global solidarity. When browsing Twitter, a disjointed vertical stripe of green seemed to appear for weeks. Just last year, social media users learned of the Haiti crisis online, and they turned social media tools into the biggest mobile phone fundraising event in history (the campaign was run by the American Red Cross). Or consider how angry iPhone 4 buyers comments and posts evoked an admission from Apple that its product had "industry-wide irregularities," and encouraged *Consumer Reports* to not recommend the product. The examples continue.

Many corporate and nonprofit executives throughout the country have awakened to the increasing power of social media and are trying to engage in this dynamic new environment. The Fifth Estate demands their attention.

Incredible amounts of user-generated information, content and entertainment now stream throughout the world's social networks. At the same time, the environment seems more dangerous as users and networks flame companies that try to spin events such as BP's horrible Deepwater Horizon eco-disaster or JetBlue's mass stranding of passengers over Valentine's Day, 2007.[12]

Given the complexity of conversational media and the dangers of a flawed strategy, executives suddenly find themselves in a quandary. They must determine how to successfully engage their company or nonprofit in social media, and quickly. The viability of their products, services and civic solutions depend on it. Yet social media successes are not created overnight. Social media programs evolve over months and years, not with a simple tweet. The tension between structured organizations' messaging and the fluid nature of conversations should not be underestimated.

This book provides organizations and executives that are struggling to adopt social media strategies for their companies with a foundation to help create them. It does not teach communicators or community managers the best way to execute a Facebook fan page, create a blogger relations program or engender a large Twitter follower count.[13] Instead, this book discusses the strategic principles and major aspects of social network marketing.

The rest of this chapter discusses the general trends driving social media and their impacts on business. Ensuing chapters discuss whether or not an organization, yours perhaps, is really ready for social media; the cultural challenges of social media adoption, listening and strategy; social media marketing; and, finally, how to stay relevant.

Social Media's Impact on Business as Usual

The first social media issue organizations must consider is negative commenting, a result of the open, transparent dialog on the Internet. "What if they publicly say our product doesn't work?" "How can they question whether their donations are being used in Africa? We are spending the money appropriately!" This fear seems endemic in an American "change-averse" business culture accustomed to controlling its brands through traditional print and broadcast messages.

With the rise of social networks, consumer trust in traditional media forms has declined dramatically. The public no longer believes as much in reporters now that there are alternative voices available to read and verify contemporary television and newspaper stories. With more choices and much more content, consumers media use patterns have shifted. Social media users are no longer beholden to one voice (often influenced by corporate marketing and PR machines) or to a limited network of contacts. It is peer-to-peer marketing at its finest, turbocharged by the viral nature of what Doc Searls calls today's Live Web.[14]

A world of experiences lies at consumers' fingertips, and many simply search to find relevant information. When they use online search engines, social media sources often are listed as top content choices. Google PageRank technology rewards content that generates conversational links. This phenomenon challenges organizational outreach efforts, disrupting traditional web marketing campaigns. On April 16, 2007, *BusinessWeek* wrote, "Trashing brands online can also be high theater."[15] Respected content brands such as Fast Company launch campaigns like the Influencer Project[16], and then find themselves lampooned within 24 hours. Millions of people watch this theater—then join in and pile on. Is it any wonder companies fear losing control of the message?

The Origin of Brands author Laura Ries said: "As quickly and as easily as PR can build a brand, PR can take a brand down. Negative PR is incredibly damaging. And with the growth of new media, mainly the Internet, it can happen faster than ever. Look no further than Don Imus, JetBlue for proof of this fact ... non-famous people or brands can be annihilated by even mild scandals. If you're not famous, you seldom get a second chance." [17]

How far will the pendulum swing? Nonprofits and businesses alike increasingly find themselves forced to communicate with their customers in the social media forms they prefer. Instead of organizations trying to find customers or donors, now organizations are trying to play catch-up with their stakeholders. For every socially engaged LIVESTRONG, there are 10 American Cancer Societies that fear the real negative whiplash an online conversation can bring.

To date, most organizational social media efforts have been limited to content publishing—like simple Twitter or Facebook updates—with mediocre results and a lack of conversations. Organizations hear about how companies and online influencers participate in social media channels and have dynamic results, then look at their own efforts and feel like they have been sold snake oil. Or worse, they see negative whiplash and are afraid to risk real engagement. As a result, there have been increasing conversations from publications like *Newsweek* about a possible social media bubble similar to the venture capital dot-com bubble of the late 20th century.[18]

This fear represents a tragedy. Organizations that leverage social media intelligently as an integrated part of their overall communications program have great things to gain, including positive relationships with loyal community members and brand advocates, better communications, new buyers or donors who consider the organization part of their communities, significant movements towards innovation or social change, increased brand loyalty and much, much more.

One of the original and most respected marketing bloggers, Toby Bloomberg, provided these insights:

Social media is more than a passive Web site strategy. The most beneficial aspect is the ability to engage directly with customers and other stakeholders. Social media opens the doors for businesses to listen to the unfiltered voices of their customers and to track those conversations. Social media also provides opportunities for the people within the company to join those conversations and talk directly to customers. Taking an active role in creating a dialogue with customers about issues that they care about, at the same moment they care about those concerns, is the heart of new media marketing.[19]

I have seen this phenomenon over and over again with brands small and large, such as Ford Motor Company's meteoric rise to online popularity (thanks to a social media team led by Scott Monty) or the amazing work The Humane Society of the United States has done integrating social media as a core part of its advocacy and fundraising efforts. Startup brands also dominate the social web like storied brands, from measuring tool Radian6's prominence among bloggers and social media communications to social media darling Charity: Water's rise to become a favorite cause amongst the Twitter community, and the ensuing donations the cause received. There are many other examples of social media enabling organizations to create valuable relationships with critical stakeholders.

This creates a big problem for corporate marketers and PR practitioners who are used to playing by the old rules and using defined methods of engagement with customers and the media. Before they could issue whatever content they wanted and it was usually accepted; communication, for the most part, could be controlled. Media are now beyond control, and content is being created by millions. Finally, organizational cultures—in the business and nonprofit sectors—revolve around stand-alone silos barred from intra department or external engagement as larger networked, transparent conversations. The new equation creates hard cultural challenges for the corporate world.

With each passing day, the gap between outdated tactics

and now's marketing needs widens. In 2007 when *Now Is Gone* was published, traditional nonprofits and companies could afford to sit on the sideline. Today, most have barren social media beachheads, publishing links and are talking with no one. Their presence is ineffective. The situation becomes more demanding as their efforts to communicate the old way fail.

It's incumbent upon organizations to learn the new social media world, not just from a theoretical level, but also as community participants. Without social media, our ability to effectively do business is incomplete. The social media revolution's impact on organizations' communications demands our professional attention.

To reach these new audiences, executives and marketing professionals must steer their organizations skillfully. To do so will require a new approach, a different mindset—one that will not only dictate the way social media is used, but also create new principles for communicating in general. Authenticity, personality and transparency—buzzwords long associated with the rise of social media—turn into new internal challenges, constantly standing as the primary pathways to increased online successes.

Case Study: Tyson Foods Hunger Relief

One of the more storied brands in cause marketing online has been Tyson Foods with its Hunger Relief program. For the past three years, the company has focused on adding value to the community of those engaged in the fight against hunger. By making use of in-kind donations and social media resources, Tyson Foods creates awareness of hunger and those involved in the issue.

Tyson has used the tools effectively, allowing the

company to be authentically engaged in the cause. In 2007, Tyson created an online presence with its Hunger Relief site, based on a WordPress site. In 2008, a Twitter account was opened (@TysonFoods) focusing on hunger relief, and in late 2009 they added a Facebook page. Images are also posted on Flickr and video on a YouTube channel.

Engagement

A central component of the company's involvement in the issue is the donation of 8 to 10 million pounds of protein to hunger- and disaster-relief efforts each year. Tyson strives to make the most of donations by creating tactics that increase awareness and engagement in the issue.

In 2008, the company began engaging Twitter users by generating donations based on Twitter activity. In the first such effort, Tyson worked with the Social Media Club of Austin (TX), 501 Tech Club of Austin and the Capital Area Food Bank of Texas. The company offered to donate 100 pounds of food, up to a 35,000 -pound truckload, for every comment on a particular blog post providing hunger statistics for the Austin area, and a connection to the food bank. The 350 comments to fill the truck were received in less than four hours, with more than 650 comments all told, and Tyson added another truckload after the first was filled. Similar efforts have occurred in Boston, New York and the San Francisco Bay area.

Tyson has also leveraged in-kind donations through two collaborative efforts with Scott Henderson, both conducted around Austin's South by Southwest Interactive festival. In 2009, Tyson, Media Sauce and others launched the Pledge to End Hunger, a virtual food drive in which a truckload of food was donated to each of five states that had the most people who went online to sign a Pledge to End Hunger.

In 2010, the effort was expanded into WeCanEndThis,

a multifaceted program that included not only the digital can drive (this time with truckload donations going to 10 states), but a cause lab at the SXSWi festival, which brought together innovative thinkers in a day-long session focused on applying new approaches to ending hunger.

Tyson also got a great number of its 107,000 domestic employees involved in the issue through an internal program branded "Powering the Spirit." In addition to volunteering with local hunger-relief providers, the employees raise funds for hunger-relief efforts in their communities.

Results

In addition to creating new awareness of hunger, Tyson has engaged the existing community of those involved in the issue, with online connections and discussion. A list of "Hunger Twitterers" was first posted on the blog in 2009 and has grown to more than 150 members. Thousands of Tyson employees have become involved in the company's hunger-relief efforts, from volunteering at local food banks to conducting fundraising efforts on behalf of hunger relief in their communities.

From a marketing perspective, the company significantly increased the online visibility of hunger-relief efforts. "Comment for Food" efforts generated more than 4,100 comments on the Tyson Hunger Relief website. The Tyson Twitter account now has more than 6,000 followers.

Their effort sparked more than 40 blog entries about the company's hunger efforts, including an "Innovative Giving" post in Fast Company.com and a piece in The Huffington Post. Online efforts have also strengthened mainstream media efforts, all of which generated more than 168 million impressions in 2009.

When asked what he thought the biggest takeways from Tyson Foods Hunger Relief effort were, Ed Nicholson, who is director of community and public relations for Tyson

Foods Inc., said: "Shine the spotlight on the cause and what others are doing, rather than yourself. It will generally reflect favorably back on you. Pound-for-pound, authentic engagement trumps cash. And you probably have resources the cause needs desperately, even if it isn't money."

The Long Tail of Media

When social media first became popular, Long Tail theory was prevalent throughout online marketing conversations. When applied, *WIRED* Editor in Chief Chris Anderson's economic theory does a great job of visualizing the ascent of new media forms in contrast with old, traditional media.[20] Since first popularized in 2004, social networks and mobile media postings have risen in the hierarchy of media.

To recap, the Long Tail theory is: With a large population of customers, their selection and buying pattern results in a power law distribution curve (Pareto distribution).[21] A market with a high freedom of choice will create a certain degree of inequality by favoring the upper 20% of the items ("hits" or "head") against the other 80% ("non-hits" or "long tail").[22]

Head of the Tail

Let's go back to the power curve for media in light of the ascendancy of some new media forms.

Hits in the Head section have the most impact (top 20% of media), while the long tail (bottom 80%) still makes up the majority of the media marketplace. This chart defines the marketplace as word-of-mouth power and readership.

This chart is subjective, and various media forms have disparate degrees of weight. General classification is the best we can do without precise measurement tools using a real-world case study with all types of earned media opportunities.

At the head of the tail are the following media forms:

- National broadcast – ABC, CBS, NBC and FOX
- Major newspapers – *New York Times, USA Today*, etc.
- Top magazines – *BusinessWeek, Fortune, WIRED*
- Major social networks – Facebook, Twitter, YouTube, Foursquare, etc.
- Top cable channels – CNN, ESPN, FOX News, etc.
- Top 100 blogs – Huffington Post, Techcrunch, Treehugger, etc.

The Turning Point and the Tail

At the turning point in the tail, roughly the 20% mark, you have several other forms of traditional media, which reflect the fall of some media and the rise of new online and mobile media.

- Major trade journals: Obviously, the powerhouses in any industry still hold sway, but the secondary journals have suffered quite a bit.
- Secondary social networks: For every Facebook there's a Gowalla. Though not as popular, these secondary networks still drive considerable traffic.
- Regional newspapers: You don't hear about the *Denver Post* much nationally. But it is still powerful in the Rocky Mountain region.

- Secondary cable and TV: A&E, TBS, VH-1, etc.
- National radio: ESPNRadio, FOX and other syndicated programming.
- Leading vertical blogs: The winner here, no question. In PR, for example, Brian Solis (who wrote *Engage* and the intro to *Now Is Gone*) will get as many or more reads as a secondary PR journal.
- Major "influencer" profiles: On some of the social networks, you have highly "influential" updates, which through mass followers or strong engagement, can set off tidal wives of action.

After that, you have the long tail, the vast majority of content. From the old world, the tail includes the following: local TV, local radio, local newspapers, secondary journals, corporate websites, e-mail newsletters and news releases. From the newer social media world, it includes social network profiles, secondary blogs, videos, photos, maps and mobile updates and check-ins.

The Taxonomy Problem

The issue with Long Tail theory is the taxonomy, which seeks to isolate individual media forms and tools and their weight. Given today's fractured media environment, one hit in any of these areas—regardless of whether it's a Fourth or Fifth Estate media form—can trigger successive hits in others. When a word-of-mouth campaign has substance, it usually cascades. Smart communicators understand this. That's why integrated outreach—not just social media or traditional PR and advertising—matters so much.

In *Now Is Gone*, we talked about this "ping-pong match" between traditional and new media outlets:

"One great way to promote your new media initiative remains traditional media, who often use well-respected blogs as sources or even the subject of stories... [Social media attention] drives information into the spotlight forcing traditional media to pay attention—or look like they've missed the news and, most importantly, the conversation. Blogs [can be] a more effective way of reaching and inspiring traditional media to react than most PR professionals and wire services combined."

Ping-pong matches demonstrate that weighting one tool by its number of readers may not be accurate. As Seth Godin said in *Meatball Sundae*, "It doesn't matter if the socially generated earned media only gets one percent of the hoped-for attention if it's the right one percent."

Another weakness in the new media environment is a degradation in the quality of information.[23] Many traditional media outlets reduced staff and have to do more with a smaller, less-experienced workforce. With blogs and influencers filling the void, general journalistic standards have suffered. While some blogs, such as Mashable, have strict editorial guidelines, others are at the whim of their authors, who may or may not have domain expertise. Discerning quality information is an important challenge for our society.

This provides an opportunity for organizations to become authoritative thought leaders if they can transition effectively from PR machines delivering messages into providers of useful factual information. To do this they must become their own "corporate journalists," their own unique form of Fifth Estate members.

Case Study: Twestival

An example of the Long Tail theories at work is Twestival, an online fundraising event run by Amanda Rose. The organized group of meet-ups uses a wide variety of social media tools to organize and promote simultaneous events in hundreds of cities across the globe, all to fundraise for charity. People throughout the world were empowered to set up their own events, show up and act on behalf of causes.

With three Twestivals in 2009 and 2010, Twestival has seen tens of thousands of people participate in charitable fundraising. Two of the fundraisers were for specific charities, charity: water and Concern, while the middle Twestival benefited charities in each host city. At the time of writing, a Twestival was being planned for 2011, again to benefit local charities.

Engagement

Twestival provides people a means to benefit a cause and the opportunity to volunteer and be a part of something bigger. They can participate in event organization or simply show up and network. Organizer Amanda Rose enforces brand and basic event guidelines and lets cities get creative with their events.

Twitter plays a primary role in outreach for the fundraising series of events. "Twitter allows a platform for organizers to shout out requests that normally might have taken weeks or months to arrange," Rose said. "Thanks to a sea of people who pass it along, a tweet might appear a few minutes, later that reads 'I can help with that.' It is extremely motivating for a local volunteer team to see the way their community pulls together to make this event a success."

Additional tools have included WhatGives!? widgets powered by PayPal linked to cities and real-time leaderboards. WordPress, Tumblr and Posterous blogs are used for local city events. GoToMeeting is used by global organizers for meetings and presentations without being in the same room, and Huddle was used with great success for online collaboration and sharing of documents.

The tools are used to foster relationships on a local level. Rose and organizers connect on the national level, too. Finally, the two specific, global charities found that they developed grassroots networks on a local level as a result of Twestival.

Results

The three Twestivals have raised more than $1.2 million through micro-donations: a small $25 cover charge, individual sponsorships and small corporate sponsorships. In addition to the $1.2 million, tens of thousands of people across the globe have attended a Twestival.

"Twestival is able to attract a large number of people because we make it a special event and different from your average meetup," Rose said. "For those attending events, I think it is really satisfying to know that every single dollar of your event is going directly to support projects — it is something people can feel good about.

"What we are asking of people with Twestival isn't just donations; it is their time, talent and resources if they want to give it. The way in which we self-organize on Twitter and other social media platforms gives us an opportunity to engage people, before and after the event, in a way that is diverse and layered. People aren't just participating in an event, they are having an impact."

"There's No Market for Messages"

In 1999, four advanced thinkers—Rick Levine, Christopher Locke, Doc Searls and David Weinberger—wrote a book called *The Cluetrain Manifesto* that touched off the online conversation revolution. At the heart of the book were 95 theses, re-purposing history's label for Martin Luther's famous rebellion against the established church, and an incredible challenge to organizational communications: "There's No Market for Messages."

In many ways, *Now Is Gone* was the product of *Cluetrain's* unrelenting view that controlled and contrived business brand messages—whether nonprofit or corporate—have no place on the Internet. *Cluetrain* represents a great hope: That business can be done differently. This viewpoint holds that the Internet and social media can become the elixir to revolutionize corporate cultures from those of exploitation as displayed by Blackwater, BP, Enron, the collapse of GM, Goldman Sachs, Halliburton and WorldComm, and refocus them on communities, responsibility, authenticity, causes and service to actual markets.

Cluetrain captures the essence of the uncontrolled business environment and the need to provide authentic dialogue based on the market's needs.[24] Without understanding the fundamental dynamics of the social media form and the inherently uncontrived two-way conversations it inspires, communicators are lost in the darkness. They no longer have control and find their messages falling on deaf ears or, worse, being publicly rejected.

The Fifth Estate does not have to accept organizational messaging. This is a fundamental struggling point that most organizations wrestle with throughout their social media adoption cycle.

It doesn't matter if you have a compelling cause or a public interest, or if your company contributes to society. If your organization relentlessly delivers messages to people, they will without doubt, turn their back on you. It's like entering a party and spamming people with solicitations, stale lines and hucksterisms.

The 20th-century, industrial approach to communications is over, regardless of medium. Mass communicating at people no longer works. We live in a networked, online communications world. Even Super Bowl ads are starting to lose strength, as evidenced by Pepsi's decision to spend $20 million instead on its social media-driven Refresh program.[25]

Whether it's social or not, organizational executives and communicators should retool their strategic approach to messaging. The old dynamics of media we learned in business or communications school, specifically the concept that people get information from limited channels of media, no longer apply.

Look at messages as conversation starters. You won't control the dialogue, but the fact of the matter is that your organization has already lost control. And some experts argue you never had it.[26] Instead, at least when it comes to online media, let's focus on having real, interesting conversations that matter to us (organizationally and personally) and to our stakeholders in online communities.

The rest of this book deals with the basics of social media and how to integrate it within a larger marketing communications effort. It assumes that a company or a practitioner has at minimum a passing interest in social media and that there's at least the possibility of engaging in a social media strategy of some form.

CHAPTER ONE SNAPSHOTS

Whether it occurs gradually or in one a moment of clarity, like mine with the Allen-Webb election, most people come to realize that social media represents a sudden shift in the way communication is taking place. A new, empowering form of communication has arisen, and it requires a completely different, grass-roots approach.

The Fifth Estate

Citizen-created content fills an information void left by the current power establishments in government, industry and the media. This new Fifth Estate keeps traditional media and power wielders accountable by pointing out fallacies and generating news that the traditional media then reports.

Impact on Organizations

Unable to "contain" negative commenting or successfully communicate in conversational media, organizations find themselves forced to change. This requires a much greater cultural adoption than simply learning new communications tools such as the fax machine or email. Now executives must unlearn decades of strategic management approaches to communications.

The Long Tail

With the exception of the most popular social networks, social media generally is not as well read as most popular forms of media. Yet the "long tail" of lightly read media can create sudden movements of information and force media leaders to report and communicate about these emerging stories. The resulting ping-pong match has created a new media ecosystem.

No Market for Messages

At the heart of corporate communications is the message, meant to be delivered, disseminated and controlled. Because of two-way communication methods, online markets reject messages, instead preferring customer feedback and opinions about products, services and solutions. At best, the role of the message in social media environments is that of a conversation-starter.

Chapter 2
Social Media Ready?

Organizations are intimidated by a Fifth Estate comprising millions of people openly expressing their opinions, sparking support and exposing weaknesses. An executive or communications professional responsible for a brand's reputation in all media forms often thinks twice before engaging. Yet companies and nonprofits risk their brands' reputation by not participating. At the same time, they risk brand degradation if they approach social media with a traditional, top-down approach rather than engaging in conversation.

Today almost every organization needs to embrace social media, even if it's just monitoring general conversation on relevant social media sites. While it's never been overtly stated, part of Apple's success stems from its responsiveness to customer feedback—positive and negative—online. Time and time again, the company has responded to social media outcries, trends and rumors. Yet, social media is no panacea, and an organization needs to understand some of the online and cultural barriers.[27]

Unfortunately, most companies and nonprofits don't consider the difficulties of participating in conversational media. Instead, they jump in because they have to or because of the perceived opportunity. While pursuing this holy Grail of public engagement, it's important to remember that monetizing social media for fundraising[28] or sales can be extremely difficult.[29] And that's assuming an organization can even wage a decent ongoing conversation. The risks of poor conversation range from wasted resources all the way to completely tarnished brands.

Social media offers organizations the means to build relationships with an extended community. It does not replace traditional marketing or communication tools, only augments them with opportunities for one-to-one (or one-to-an influential few) engagement.

The next step is to integrate regular tools and approaches that allow willing community members to take actions (vote, buy, donate, volunteer.). Look at the Humane Society's website (http://www.humanesociety.org/) and all the things visitors can do immediately on their social outlets. How an organization uses social media to facilitate its business becomes a unique thing tied directly to its mission.

Organizations should consider several crucial preliminary steps before employing social media:
 •   Listen and understand how social media tools fit into an organization's larger stakeholder ecosystem.

• Get ready to give up control of the message. This is a huge barrier for many executives, who have been steeped in command-and-control communications training.

• Make sure the organization can commit the financial and human resources necessary.

• Get real. Personal relationships like those developed through social media require ethics and authenticity that an organization must offer.

• Understand how to manage the dangers of personal branders and personalities on the Internet.

This is a difficult set of challenges. Committing to social media requires embarking on a cultural journey that, like it or not, will change the organization internally. Even storied social media brands like Dell went through incredible journeys to embrace their customers with crowdsource initiatives. Crowdsourcing is the process of outsourcing work to an unspecified group of people usually for free or for a contest prize with a general public appeal on the Internet. The ability for thousands of people to openly express their opinions—externally and internally—is intimidating. Whether or not a company or nonprofit participates in this open environment —or, more likely, its degree of participation—requires strategic decisions.

It's important to remember that competitors, success with social media will encourage organizations to participate openly or lose market share. Authors Don Tapscott and Anthony Williams did a great job encapsulating this trend in their book *Wikinomics*. This book, which began as a $9 million research project, went into great detail describing how online communities and group contributions benefit businesses.

The result, according to book reviewer Joe Wikert: "While

some leaders fear the heaving growth of these massive online communities, *Wikinomics* proves this fear is folly. Smart firms can harness collective capability and genius to spur innovation, growth, and success." [30]

But it's not a light-bulb moment or as easy as starting a Facebook page or Twitter profile. For almost every organization, social media is an evolutionary process that not only organically builds a community on the outside, but also changes its internal culture. [31]

Case Study: BP Meets @BPGlobalPR

During the height of the Deepwater Horizon oil spill—the largest ever on record—BP deployed a series of social media and paid online search advertising campaigns to sway public opinion toward its responsible approach in cleaning up the oil. The media largely ignored the oil spill at first, and the Obama administration trusted BP to clean it up. However, bloggers kept raising questions, publishing stories of malfeasance and highlighting the damage of the oil spill that began on April 20, 2010.

BP largely ignored these social media outcries on its public social media channels on Facebook and Twitter. When you have a two-way channel like Facebook or Twitter, you're expected to have a conversation. You have to embrace everyone, positive AND negative. When people feel ignored, their anger just grows. And that's exactly what BP found out—broadcasting and not talking created a firestorm of anger in the form of @BPGlobalPR.

Engagement

An anonymous tweeter (who chose the pseudonym Leroy Stick) using the Twitter handle @BPGlobalPR appeared. Stick ridiculed BP's social media with posts like:

"Cleaning up oil spills is expensive. Buying judges so we can keep drilling? Relatively cheap." The onslaught of BP ads claiming responsibility became the subject matter of Stick's ridicule, and the ensuing groundswell that surrounded @BPGlobalPR's tweets burst the oil spill into the news across the blogosphere.

In his one major public discussion of his actions (Leroy Stick is an anonymous handle), Stick explained his motives: "I started @BPGlobalPR because the oil spill had been going on for almost a month and all BP had to offer were bullshit PR statements. No solutions, no urgency, no sincerity, no nothing. That's why I decided to relate to the public for them."

Communications pundits have chased their own tails analyzing the impact of Stick's efforts. One thing remains certain: BP can't tweet its way into good graces. [32]

Results

At the time of writing, BP's official Twitter handle @BP_America had 18,000 followers, and @BPGlobalPR had 189,000 followers. Stick's faux BP account had inspired more than 60,000 blog impressions on Google Blogsearch. The media coverage of BP's malfeasance escalated in May and June and forced the Obama administration to call BP's global management team in from the UK and dedicate a $20 billion fund to pay damages. CEO Tony Hayward eventually lost his job.

An argument can be made that Stick and the groundswell of supporters and bloggers that rallied around him did more to hold BP and the Obama administration accountable online than any other organization or entity. In Beth Kanter and Allison Fine's new book The *Networked Nonprofit*, they talk about the concept of "free agents," individuals who crash into the walls of traditional nonprofits using social media tools. These agents force change by breaking control paradigms and having conversations with people, building their own movements.

As Leroy Stick demonstrates, the free-agent concept goes beyond the nonprofit world and extends to the larger social media ethos. His @BPGlobalPR effort represented free agency and the Fifth Estate's fierce independence at its most powerful levels. @BPGlobalPR forced BP into accountability.

Listen First

Have you ever joined a conversation among strangers at a party and start talking right away, only to find them drifting away? No one likes to have their conversation interrupted. Normal etiquette is to walk up, listen, introduce yourself, perhaps ask a question, and then participate after listening for a few minutes.

But what do most organizations do when they first engage on the social web? Butt in and start talking. It's almost as if venues such as Facebook, Twitter and YouTube have turned into shouting matches featuring organizations' latest statements, messages or random facts. The worst practice is posting news releases as links for presumed readers. Is it any wonder that organizations struggle to generate significant followings online, then conclude that social media doesn't work?

Many organizations are not used to listening. In a mass communications world, they've done most of the talking.

Social media communities present a different set of rules. Two-way communication allows stakeholders to have equal footing with businesses and organizations. The Fifth Estate does not have to yield attention to business; their decision to interact with organizations is strictly on an opt-in basis. Organizations' failure to listen to the larger community creates situations where stakeholders either react with anger or simply tune out.[33]

The realization that your nonprofit or company is part of something bigger is a huge breakthrough for most executives and communicators. Manish Mehta, vice president of community at Dell, likened it to Nicolaus Copernicus' 16th-century revelation that displaced the concept of the Earth as the center of the universe.[34]

The intelligence an organization gathers from listening to social media conversations provides market research. The public conversation happens with or without your organization's participation, so you may as well reap the benefits of at least passively monitoring it. The intelligence gathered can include, but is not limited to, product awareness, sensitivity toward social issues, motivations, trends in product features like geolocation, political trends, and much more. Savvy organizations can turn dynamic conversations into virtual focus groups, then turn the resulting intelligence into new, dynamic messages that serve as provocative conversation-starters. Exit those old, boring news releases.

The benefits of listening don't stop there.

A recent Forrester report showed that some social media listening platforms have evolved to the point that attentive organizations use them to address such diverse marketing and business functions as campaign measurement, market research, customer support and sales enablement.[35] Organizations can set up free monitoring platforms using Google, search on major social networks and other functions, or they can deploy paid services to gather the intelligence in a managed platform. Currently, according to the Forrester report, the top paid platforms are Converseon, Nielsen and Radian6.

They are leading because of their range of product functionality and their ability to meet businesses' needs beyond reactive brand tracking. [36]

Giving Up Control of the Message

The first thing communicators must understand is that they cannot control a message within social networks. Members of the Fifth Estate may willingly or subconsciously adopt a message, but this is not controllable. Communication must resonate with the community for it to work. At best we can attract influencers and community members to the conversation we hope to inspire. The ensuing dialogue may provide unexpected insights about an organization.

JetBlue was absolutely lambasted when it failed to cancel flights and left passengers sitting on runways for many hours during a Valentine's Day storm in 2007. Instead of communicating with the public about this issue (for example, detailing what the airline was doing to resolve its problems), the then popular JetBlue blog went silent, and traditional media relations were employed to communicate during the crisis. The blogosphere went crazy. JetBlue sported a social network black eye for months. Here's a comment from Social Media Group Founder Maggie Fox on a "60 Days Later, What Do You Think" posted on Shel Israel's popular Global Neighborhoods blog[37] :

I feel about the same about JetBlue–that they're a great, cheap way to fly to NYC. In fact, week after next I'll be on one of their planes. However, if they leave us sitting on the tarmac for 3 hours, my perception will change completely and I will hate them utterly.

So maybe this is how things have changed: before they might have had 2 or 3 chances to make mistakes before I disliked them as an airline. Now they have none.

JetBlue's attempt to control its message in the old, traditional way after engaging its constituency with a blog demonstrates that social networks cannot be turned on and off at will. This is a dramatic shift for communications professionals who have been trained to control the message.

Before the social media revolution, the biggest danger to an organization was when the media seized on a negative, headline-grabbing situation. "Bad coverage," it was called. In a typical negative scenario, a person started a grassroots campaign to draw attention to an organization's ills, attracting traditional media coverage and bad word of mouth. The worst-case scenario occurred when fact-based scandals such as Enron broke out, or with massive product recalls. Now every customer and donor is free to comment, each with the potential of going viral.

It's not surprising that social networks can't be contained because they mirror human relationships. Most people detest being controlled. Ever try to buy a new car, only to be confronted by an aggressive salesperson at the dealership? It's a most uncomfortable feeling, a transaction devoid of relationship-oriented conversation.

However, people will listen to a genuine conversation. They'll allow you to influence them, and they'll give your argument or product or service a chance as long as you take their needs and desires into consideration. Social media means creating a relationship of trust with an extended community beyond the organization's walls. If the community feels that trust is broken, for whatever reason (e.g., Bill Clinton's "I did not have sex with that woman," or BP's insincere commitment to openly communicate about the Deepwater Horizon oil spill), there's a whiplash effect that destroys credibility.

This change in communication strategy requires a huge cultural shift for any organization more than ten years old. It's so dramatic that the entire next chapter has been devoted to the topic. The organizational, cultural challenges of social media have by far been the biggest barrier to companies success.

Members of the Fifth Estate are no longer beholden to monolithic, traditional media forms. They can use new media to state their views—right or wrong. They don't have to submit facts to a managing editor, and they don't need to run corrections. Companies' controlling the message is a luxury of times past. Further, social media influence is based on trust, so now more than ever, true relationship building is thrust upon corporations and nonprofits. This means they have to be honest, communicate, give as well as take, and be prepared for feedback.

It forces high-ranking executives to jump back into customer relations, helping to foster dialogue between the people who make up the customer base and the people at the company. It's creating a new level of customer service, which now is being called social Customer Relations Management or sCRM online.

Giving up control is not a bad thing—in fact it's less about "giving up" and more about embracing a larger extended enterprise and welcoming interested community loyalists into the fold. It injects a new step into the marketing process, which, by default, makes it more transparent and genuine.

Consider the valuable lessons that Southwest Airlines got from its online community when there was a very negative reaction to the possibility of assigned seating. New seating arrangements (the familiar poles we all see at Southwest gates across the country) were created that met loyal customer desires, as well as enabled new business-class revenue structures. As a result of listening to negative feedback, the airline was able to address its customers' wants and needs, and at the same time make them feel engaged with the airline.[38] Lack of control worked to Southwest's benefit.

Does the Organization Have the Capacity to Participate?

The difference between organizational brand promotion and community marketing is similar to broadcasting versus talking, listening and responding. With the rise of social networks in the past few years, the audience has become a community, and instead of talking at its members, one must converse with them. That means that within social media forms, the mass promotion takes on a more Zen-like approach to attracting customers through grassroots community participation.

No one better stated this than Jay Rosen in his PressThink article, "The People Formerly Known as the Audience":

You don't own the eyeballs. You don't own the press, which is now divided into pro and amateur zones. You don't control production on the new platform, which isn't one-way. There's a new balance of power between you and us. The people formerly known as the audience are simply the public made realer, less fictional, more able, less predictable.[39]

Even traditional mass advertising is changing, influenced by new media forms around it. KFC has run advertising campaigns with promotional codes embedded in each commercial to drive people to the KFC online community. Doritos ran Super Bowl advertising segments generated by Doritos fans. Pepsi has turned its social giving program into an online mega contest called Refresh that features crowdsourced initiatives suggested by individuals within and chosen by the Fifth Estate.

Instead of standing on a speaker box and dictating propaganda to your audience, it's now time to get into the street and interact with your community—one by one by one. This is an attitude difference, but it's also a capacity issue. Returning to relationships requires time. What traditional communications department has the time to respond to comments, Tweets, Facebook questions and a wide variety of media?

While this may seem like a resource imposition, in reality it's a return to old-fashioned values. Relationships and values in the sense of the baker, the butcher and general store owner down on Main Street. People want to know their vendors, they want to interact with them. Most importantly, they want to be heard! And now, the small-town feel is a global phenomenon existing in millions of global micro-communities.

Most organizations create or reallocate a portion of someone's time for a community manager position. This person's job is to facilitate online conversations and community development. In fact, ReadWriteWeb has created a Guide to

Online Community Management to share best practices based on early experiences on the social web.[40] Other organizations choose several players to engage online, sharing the load and creating redundancy.

Creating a community manager within your organization requires a real resource commitment. Participation within a community means more than publishing a link on Facebook or a tweet on Twitter. It requires listening to other conversations, making consistent blog posts (if your organization chooses to blog), commenting on other organizational and individual social media posts, as well as dynamic interaction on your chosen social networks. The effort can be quite time-consuming.

In a MarketingProfs interview with Michael Stelzner, Pete Blackshaw, then CMO of Neilsen BuzzMetrics, said: "I love my blog and its topic, but frankly, I'm struggling to keep up. I'm just not cranking out content like I used to, and feel as if I'm contributing 'too little, too late.' I'm starting to freak about folks potentially sending unsubscribe pings my way, and I just can't handle the thought of such rejection... Creating great and compelling online content takes real work and commitment."[41]

If a company fails to allocate resources and build capacity necessary to launch a social media presence, the result will more than likely be a stalled initiative. The Internet is littered with un-updated social accounts, dead blogs and listless communities floundering from lack of attention.

To succeed means setting aside financial resources for things like personnel (an individual's time or more), blog templates, custom widgets to aggregate social network content, web design, and more. It means allocating time, and often not just the community manager's. Others across the organization may need to participate. And finally, it takes real thought about your stakeholders and the organization's mission. Vapid social media rarely works. So from a resource perspective, it is not something to dump on the college intern. Senior leadership needs to be involved.

In some ways, it would be better not to start at all than to push a big social media effort that simply disappears or, worse, stops with un-updated social network profiles, a static blog or a non-participating avatar (a.k.a. the daily message from the ivory tower on Facebook or Twitter). Most mature community members have seen these failed starts from organizations and thus are skeptical of newer entities online. There is increasingly a wait-and-see period for newer players. A business or nonprofit must truly commit to social media if it wants to succeed with it.

Case Study: Miriam's Kitchen

I first encountered the Miriam's Kitchen, a kitchen serving Washington DC's homeless citizens, during the summer of 2009 when the D.C. organizing committee selected the Kitchen as its charity of choice for the second Twestival. At the time, we felt they would make the most from the exposure, and I think we sold them short. Their ability to grasp online social relationships and extend them to real life actions has been outstanding. It's an honor to feature Miriam's Kitchen as a case study.

Miriam's Kitchen decided to participate in online media because many of their supporters were using social media. It's important that we meet our supporters where they are, and social media helps us accomplish this. Many of the Washington, D.C., residents who donate and volunteer fall within the 25-40 age range and are social media/web savvy.

"We also connect with some of our homeless guests through social media," said Jennifer Roccanti, development associate and Miriam's Kitchen's primary voice on the web. "While interactions online are rare, a few of our guests have posted messages to us on our Facebook page, and some of them have started using Twitter. We recently heard from our case managers that a few guests check our Facebook page for the daily menu before they decide whether or not to make the couple-mile trek to Miriam's Kitchen each day. That's a lot of pressure on our social media team."

Engagement

Like many nonprofits, Miriam's Kitchen doesn't have many resources, and most people there have multiple jobs. The 501c(3) uses Twitter and Facebook primarily (with a dash of YouTube) as part of a larger communications strategy. The Kitchen provides daily updates on these sites, specifically what it is serving that day, while encouraging local community members to participate via recognition and interaction.

The organization has successfully engaged many of D.C.'s most influential digital voices. From the AARP social media team to Chris Abraham, these voices celebrate being a part of the extended Miriam's Kitchen family with public declarations of support.

The Kitchen also receives tremendous support from people across the country who have found it through online channels, an unintended benefit of its social communications. "We've connected with people we wouldn't have otherwise, and amazing things have happened because of those connections," Roccanti said.

Results

"The measurable outcome we are most concerned with

right now is deepening relationships with our supporters," Roccanti added. "It's been a challenge to measure that outcome, but some indicators of our success include raising more money than ever in 2009, raising more money online than ever before in 2009, and raising $10,000 through the Washington, D.C., Twestival in 2009."

The Kitchen also points toward anecdotal evidence of deepened relationships through the use of social media. Whether it be through volunteers becoming more engaged, donors seeing the impact of their donations and then increasing their gifts, or guests feeling part of its online community—social media has brought Miriam's Kitchen countless benefits in the past two years.

Personal Relations Mean Ethics and Transparency

In a medium that centers on conversations, deeper loyalty and relationships are the goal for organizations. At the heart of deeper relationships is trust, and given the low trust that many people hold for corporations and government (nonprofits generally fare better), forging strong relations means demonstrating ethics and transparency in relationships.[42]

This is a touchy requirement, but it is a crucial one. An organization must be what it represents itself to be, or it risks great peril with its social-media-based online communities.

A brand is a commitment, a promise to your community. It also is an evolving entity that, now more than ever, is co-created by its community of customers and stakeholders. A brand is represented three ways; the first two are visually (ads, creative, website) and verbally (written word, website, oral communications). The third way is the most important — the experience. If the experience does not match the promotion's verbal and visual portrayal, then the community feels betrayed and the brand develops a bad reputation. Once a brand falls into ill repute, it is very hard to recover trust.

The social media world has little tolerance for organizations that aren't authentic in their representation. Internet users already suspect corporate America, so social media initiatives often are on a shorter leash. Most people are not interested in being part of a community that tolerates or enables unethical behavior.

As an example, many companies today take blogging for granted; they blog out of imagined necessity instead of realizing it as a bigger opportunity to enhance social customer relations management (sCRM). Most online communities expect some level of transparency of corporate members' activities. This type of trust demands that corporate and nonprofit entities behave in the community's interest. There is a level of tolerance for human error, but an organization must be sincere and act ethically, communicating how it is resolving those errors to the benefit of all.

If an organization does not communicate transparently during times of crisis (the JetBlue and BP examples), then it will not be well regarded by online community participants. Its social communications lose stature and become the subject of negative comments, and eventually (or immediately, depending on the situation) its brand reputation can erode. In short, if a company or nonprofit has not traditionally been open in its dialogue with customers, its culture may not be social-media ready. An organization has to be ready to take both the good and the bad of online conversations.

Further, if the organization has a history of ethics issues or its work is top secret, then social media complaints should be expected, based if nothing else on public suspicion. While it may be a good idea to strive for restored public trust, there will be little immediate marketing value from such an effort. Here are some examples of behavior that may cause distrust:

- Julian Assange's accused personal behavior juxtaposed with his heroic positioning of Wikileaks
- BP's actions in Deep Horizon and the ensuing online communications about oil spill
- Donald Rumsfeld and his actions as Defense Secretary (now on Twitter)
- LeBron James (also on Twitter) and his half hour ESPN special announcing his decision to take his "talents to Miami."

Trust needs to be fostered through strong ethical action in social networks of any kind. Without actions to back up the talk, there's little hope of success. It's better to invest in becoming a more trustworthy culture before engaging in media that require trust.

The Organizational Dangers of Personal Brands

The trust factor is why personality is so important in social communications. Personality—the people behind the communications—creates windows into the soul of the company or nonprofit. Personality is at the heart of social communications. It must be included—and backed up by the right actions—if people are going to trust the organization's communications.[43]

Personal voices in the form of community managers, blog authors and Twitter representatives have been a source of great consternation for organizations. Instead of speaking as an entity, now individuals within the entity become its public faces. That requires a new level of empowerment of and trust for communicators who are used to command-and-control messaging.

This tension between personal voices and their corporate and nonprofit employers has been felt for almost a decade. An important example is Robert Scoble, whose video blog Channel 8 had an incredibly humanizing effect on Microsoft's image toward the end of the Bill Gates era.[44] At the same time, many communicators perceived Scoble's departure as a big loss for Microsoft, and a demonstration of the potential damage personal branding can bring to an organization's communications effort.[45]

Some individual social media luminaries relish and nurture their personal brands. Beyond the obvious narcissism[46] and the off-center marketing theory behind this pop ethos,[47] organizations need to be wary of allowing personal brands to undermine their social media efforts.

The dangers range from the obvious to hidden effects. Here are some of the top ones:

• A departure by the brand personality creates an irreplaceable void. Worse, the online community, one built using the brand's time and resources, departs with "the star" because followers are vested in the individual, not the organization.[48]

• Personal transgressions not only tarnish the individual but also the nonprofit or company backing it.[49]

• Stakeholders only want to interact with the personality, rather than more qualified organization members (depending on the request).[50]

• Internal voices get angry with the personal brand for

seeking to dominate online media or becoming the center of attention..[51]

• Inauthentic use of a personality to represent a "social" brand becomes apparent as people try to interact with the organization elsewhere and find that departmental barriers still exist.[52]

This creates a dilemma for companies: The need to employ personality and conversation in their online communications rather than control or stifle individual voices. Leaning toward freedom of expression is the necessary middle path, while the company can be protected with savvy communications guidelines and human-resource approaches. Creating guidelines and rules of engagement are critical aspects of cultural adoption (covered in the next chapter).

Teams

From a human resource capacity perspective, team social media approaches resolve the personality conundrum.[53]

It's important to note that online you will always have individuals propelling brands into the spotlight, and inadvertently become stars in their own right. However, the best corporate social media strategies offer teams of people interacting on the Internet. Consider some of the biggest winners so far: Dell and the Humane Society. Some personalities naturally rising to the top. They are the stars (for example, Dell's Lionel Menchaca or Richard Binhammer), and every winning team has stars.

Yet they are still team players who intentionally focus on the organization rather than building a personal brand. Furthermore, all team members are allowed and empowered to excel.

Community-centric Management

Beyond team approaches, the purpose of social media should be fostering community. In that sense, social media efforts for great brands foster loyalty within the community, not an individual's or a company's brand. When it becomes personality or brand-focused, a community becomes rudderless.

A personality-laden brand that handles this well is the LIVESTRONG community, a brand of the Lance Armstrong Foundation. In addition to the overarching presence of Armstrong, lively LIVESTRONG participants include CEO Doug Ulman and community manager Brooke McMillan. Yet, throughout the social media tools it employs LIVESTRONG's focus is clearly on community, from its Gowalla mobile check-ins to its blog.

The best way to manage community expectations versus personal branding (beyond hiring well) is with well-structured social media guidelines. These guidelines should be community-centric in their approach. Communications staffers who use social media tools should be trained in, and reviewed regarding their use of these guidelines. Our next chapter goes more in depth on developing guidelines.

CHAPTER 2 SNAPSHOTS

Many organizations don't want to engage the Fifth Estate, or when they enter into a community they do so without considering the implications participation can have on the organization's culture. There are several critical aspects of social media an organization should consider before jumping in.

Listening Comes First

Most organizations don't listen to their stakeholders, often thinking that they already understand their needs and wants before engaging with them. But by listening first, organizations best prepare themselves to become a part of a larger conversation and community. In many ways, listening becomes a form of market research.

Message Control

Organizational control of the message does not exist in social network environments. Social network users often comment about a company or nonprofit's perceived flaws despite its traditional media coverage or official statements. By taking stakeholders' concerns into account, organizations can better develop communications and address feedback accordingly, thus bolstering their regard in the social media world.

Creating Capacity to Succeed

Success in social media requires relationships and conversations developed during a continual presence. That means staffing an organization to succeed. A corporate or nonprofit staff must diligently engage the community with appealing content on an ongoing basis, not just for the first few months.

Ethics and Transparency

A brand is a promise to the community, and relationships are the stock and trade of social media founded on trust. If the public's trust is broken by an organization misrepresenting itself, regaining it will be difficult. The Fifth Estate expects an organization to represent itself ethically online and demonstrate transparency in organizational efforts, especially in crisis situations.

The Organizational Dangers of Personal Brands

Creating trust requires adding human voices and personalities to organizations' social media efforts. At the same time, the infusion of personality-driven media online has created a phenomenon described as personal branding. The creation of personal within its social media presence poses dangers for an organization. Team and organization-focused community approaches, while still enabling individual personality and expression, can obviate many of these dangers.

Chapter 3
Becoming the Fifth Estate

In the past, media relations operations took a top-down messaging approach to communications. Only assigned spokespeople were permitted to talk with the media or in public on behalf of an organization. Advertising and other forms of public outreach were the domain of the communications staff.

Now, online social networks are creating a world in which mass media approaches no longer work, because increasingly, they fall on deaf ears. With fewer traditional media and more disparate sources of information, stakeholders are more resistant to the usual corporate communications efforts. As Greg Verdino has stated in his book, *MicroMarketing*, it's an era of micromedia, which, in turn, requires micromarketing.

Many organizations have tried to engage in social media with mixed results. Often, the inability to embrace the conversational tone necessary for social success grows from the organizations' cultural processes. Many processes are built to minimize the likelihood of a public embarrassment with the media, prevent the damages of downloading viruses on computers, and to protect trade secrets. Together, communications, IT and legal departments have become sources to protect an organization's integrity.

Industrial-era corporate structures built to protect have created departments that wield almost absolute domain over their subject areas, cripple online efforts.[54] Start with legal and executive departments' command and control methods toward communications and add IT department controls over Internet use and software. By the time an organization offers an approved communication to its stakeholders, the effort offers little relevance or conversation that interests Fifth Estate members.

To be effective, an organization has to transform its culture to participate nimbly in social media communities. It has to undergo several changes, the first of which is to change its approach toward online communicating. A top-down approach does not work. The Fifth Estate demands a deeper level of authenticity.

An organization needs to become a community member, literally a part of the Fifth Estate. It can be tough for executives and communicators to swallow this concept, but in reality the Fifth Estate already exists within its walls! As the Air Force so aptly puts it, every airman is a communicator.[55] The sooner companies and nonprofits embrace social media—not just as a communications tool but as a factual reality that permeates its very culture—the easier adoption will become.

Greg Verdino writes: "When a company attempts to interrupt the stream, the stream is bound to shift course, or simply flow around the interruption. But if a brand can actually become part of the stream, it will be carried along in the flow itself."[56]

This community-centric approach to communicating in social networks involves a commitment to create a social media policy across the organization so that online conversations can occur freely.[57] It helps to develop an embedded journalistic approach toward providing information.[58] By building relationships with individual members of the community, and offering factual, quality and relevant information, organizations become vital members of the Fifth Estate.

Consider how the American Red Cross has approached its effort to evolve emergency social data communications—requests for help on social networks—during a crisis. Rather than issue a news release, ARC's executive and communications team asked 150 community members to participate in a conference in person, and thousands more participated virtually. It published blog posts and research to provide information in advance of the conference, and it is taking community input on a wiki and through roundtables to develop new approaches to social media requests for help.[59]

This effort-in-progress is an example of embracing and becoming a part of the Fifth Estate. ARC participates within a larger conversational ecosystem. But to get there, ARC had to do more than just have the right attitude. It has evolved its culture significantly for several years. During that period, the ARC established processes for social fundraising, employee communications and online public relations (In fact, the organization's social media successes were a case study in my previous book, *Now Is Gone*).

My colleague Beth Kanter calls this cultural shift becoming "networked." [60] Instead of simply launching a campaign or an initiative, first turning the focus inward and examining cultural barriers can yield much greater success. This chapter continues by discussing these issues:

- Cultural silos in organizations
- Management and communicators need to make an adjustment
- Moving from silos to hives: Optimizing processes
- Creating social media policies

These four points are crucial to transforming your organization into an effective, networked member of the Fifth Estate.

Case Study: Madonna versus Lady Gaga

The difference between traditional approaches and the new social two-way approaches toward communications can best be typified by a couple of stars that all of us can recognize: Madonna and Lady Gaga. Analyzing their brands and networked phenomena reveals two very different approaches to social media and results.

Madonna's Engagement

Madonna is an branding genius. She is able to transform and reinvent herself decade after decade and stay relevant. Her 2008 album "Hard Candy" was a No. 1 bestseller, the seventh of her 27-year career. Yet Madonna is not a huge social media success. The branding doesn't translate. The reasons are clear when you examine her community page, which reads: "Please note that posting

Madonna unreleased material (including photos, audio and video) to your profile is not allowed. Doing so could result in the immediate termination of your membership with Icon."

Madonna is in control, messaging at her stakeholders. Her image is complete, and her content quality secure. As a result, no one really wants to talk about her in conversational media forms. Given how she has controlled her community, is it any wonder?

Lady Gaga's Engagement

Lady Gaga engages in networked communications, encouraging her "Little Monsters" in real dialogue on Twitter and elsewhere. She empowers them, too, letting them take her content and re-purpose it any way they want to. If they make a recording at a show, they can post it online without fear of reprisal (reminiscent of the Grateful Dead's longtime embracing of their community). She has done everything in the face of the recording industry's usual command-and-control approach to marketing artists.

As Citizen Marketer author Jackie Huba noted in a case study, Lady Gaga has built a magnificent global network of Little Monsters. As Huba's analysis makes clear, Lady Gaga has done that methodically:

— She gave her fans a name;

—Lady Gaga made Little Monsters bigger than her self, creating a larger ecosystem;

—She offers her stakeholders shared symbols, and content, too;

—She makes her customers feel like they also are stars;

—Lady Gaga uses social media tools to achieve these networked community objectives[61]

Results

Both women are brilliant artists. They both get the stark, wild sexy imagery that captivates their fans. It's fair to say that while Lady Gaga doesn't have the brand track record of Madonna, she understands branding. Of the two, only one has transcended traditional media success to become an online hit—Lady Gaga.

Lady Gaga owns the current record for the most viewed YouTube video in history, quickly approaching 200 million views:. Is it any wonder that Lady Gaga's first six singles, good or bad, like them or hate them, have gone straight to No. 1? Lady Gaga has transcended 20th-century marketing to become one of the first major music brands of the 21st century. Unlike Madonna or other command-and control-organizations, it's about making it easy for people to embrace the Lady Gaga brand and run with it.

A Question of Culture and Silos

It seems as if every organization in America wrestles with social media adoption. In 2008, a running joke was that more than 60,000 social media experts exist on Twitter to help companies and nonprofits engage. Yet the first era of corporate social media has been marred by astounding failure rates, as high as 70, 80 and even 90 percent, according to analysts at firms such as Forrester and eMarketer.[62] [63]

When dissecting the "Great Social Failure," observers such as David Armano, Beth Kanter and Charlene Li examine organizational cultures. While many pundits like to blame message control, these commentators say the depth of online antisocial behavior is rooted in the cultural structures of today's corporations and nonprofits. Organizations are confounded by their own industrial structures, which are manifest in departmental silos and legal policies designed to ensure workflow and protect the organization from getting sued.[64]

There's no greater example than the enormous challenges the Obama administration is faces moving the government into the Web 2.0 era. No one questions whether the Obama administration understands social media. The 2008 election often is considered the benchmark of political social communications. But federal agencies shy away from getting publicly lambasted, which prevents them from openly adopting online conversations.[65]

The social media change could be regarded as part of an overall corporate management shift caused by the information revolution. This began with the wide-scale deployment of the World Wide Web and e-mail in the 1990s. That revolution is rendering industrial corporate structures obsolete, forcing extended networks of information flow, which in turn has created decentralized workforces, suppliers and distribution networks.

It makes sense that corporate communications would follow the Fifth Estate with two-way interaction. The communications movement toward social media represents a natural progression of the information age. As such, corporate structures are straining to adapt, just as they did in the 90s. Consider how human resources departments have had to move toward talent-management principles to remain relevant in an era of widespread information.

Many companies attempt social media as a trial balloon. While this short-term approach can be successful and represents a way to introduce the power of social media, it does not build an organization that can truly engage with the Fifth Estate.

Silos are the departments that industrial-era organizations build to delegate work and ensure subject matter expertise. Human resources, public affairs or communications, development or sales, and legal are all examples of common silo departments in larger organizations. In an effort to ensure their expertise, organizations have built procedures and rules to prevent internal parties from acting without permission. This has created slow organizations that often opt for benign communications that remove any realistic opportunity for customer contact, feedback or dialog.

The siloization of social media within communications departments and their agencies represents a profound strategic error.[66] If social media is truly the interaction of people, and the exchange of their information and cultural values, then you can't put people in a box and expect success. Culture rarely subsists successfully in a container.[67] Neither does communication, which is often nimble and moves rapidly between on- and offline social networks. Integration with other communication methods is the key.

Silos prevent people from empowering the edges of their stakeholder networks. Here are the top five silos your organization will face as it moves to adopt:

1) Executive Suite—Increasingly, executives understand that they should be engaged in social media, both for customer relations and for internal morale and engagement. Yet, they seem to want to relegate social media to a single department or to a young staffer, rather than to look at how organizations are using social media to transform their businesses and

nonprofits in the modern era.[68] As a result, when issues arise, executives seem not to care much about changing policies to allow departments to work together in a more fluid manner. By its very nature, social media will challenge organizations to collaborate in unthought-of ways in a rapid fashion.

2) Communications—Control, control, control. A business function that was meant to build good relationships between people has instead evolved into controlling the message. Telling people what they want to hear or sticking to your three messages, truthful or not, is a common practice. Faced with social media, PR practitioners need to unlearn, retrain and change. Agencies have a very hard time with this because in order to be authentic, the customers need to communicate directly with organizations not just to a media relations representative. This undermines the traditional industry model.

3) IT— Another industry dramatically affected by social media is information technology, or IT. Communications technology is faster, cheaper and more efficient now. Changes include integrating open APIs, evolving security structures to meet peer-to-peer activity, and rapidly evolving databases to allow for cross-pollination across departments (sales and marketing/development to PR to customer service). It's difficult adapting so many IT execs find it easier to hide behind a policy and say no.[69]

4) Sales and Marketing (or Development)—This department likes social media, as long as it turns into hard return on investment (ROI). This is understandable, but social media is a relationship-driven medium. It requires a balance of patience and well-integrated, soft calls-to-action to deliver ROI. Many financially driven managers do not have the patience for the

organic nature of this process and can create errors in an attempt to drive numbers.

5) Legal—The group that seems likely to be most difficult is the one that seems to be a lesser evil in the equation. While there certainly are implications to consider, overall, attorneys seem to get that it is in the organization's best interest to use social media.[70] Many are able to create policies and disclaimers that protect the organization while freeing it to participate. This gets thorny quickly, though, with a public issue in which the organization might be found liable, or for highly regulated businesses or organizations (for example, hospitals).

Management and Communications
Need an Attitude Adjustment

The two silos that must change first are the executive management team and the communications department. Management should bring more voices to the table. The internal battles to prevent social networked communications across departmental domains will be significant. Many entrenched executives rely on the safe and the known. They seek to protect their power, and cultural change often requires authority greater than theirs within the organization. Top-down support for social media adoption is essential.

The Humane Society of the United States is often cited as a top nonprofit using social media, in large part because of CEO Wayne Pacelle's leadership. In addition to his own social media efforts, Pacelle encourages the entire organization to participate in social media on behalf of the Humane Society, making it an intrinsic part of their activities as members of the Fifth Estate. In addition to its seven-member, online communications department, program managers and volunteer activists routinely operate on behalf of HSUS.

This does not mean crowdsourcing your finances and trade secrets. It does acknowledge that real conversations involve more stakeholders than just the people inside the walls of the department, division or organization. It means embracing the Fifth Estate —— not as a group of meddling intruders, but as other people just like you, people expect a genuine relationship with your organization using social media tools.

If you are afraid of what will happen, here are a few thoughts for you:

• Competitors will read your conversations. They will see what you are doing. And in most cases their efforts to emulate you will fail because they are not you, and while you are open, your core offering is unique to your people and processes.

• Customers and partners will want to suggest that products, services or programs be run differently. And you know what? Some of their ideas could improve your company or lead you in new directions.

• The integrity of the company and internal relationships will not be diminished. You will not lose power. Instead you will strengthen relationships and add more human capital and equity.

There are many case studies and books about the power of social media and the results it can achieve.[71] Now it's a question of whether the team of lead executives, including the CEO, COO, CFO, CMO, etc. (the C-suite) is willing to embrace the difficult change to become a socially engaged enterprise. The C-suite needs to take responsibility for moving the cultural bar toward openness. A decision means nothing without ensuing action to change the way relational communications are approached throughout the organization.

From a communications department perspective, an attitude adjustment could greatly benefit organizations. Instead of always showing a shiny, happy picture or offering top-down messages, there's a need to get into the metaphorical streets and become members of the community.

Case in point: Consider one automaker which has experienced troubles recently. Toyota's USA Facebook fan page seems like a veritable lovefest and you would be tempted at first glance to think it was wonderful. But as you scroll through, you see that no one from Toyota is communicating. When rare negative messages appear, a post from a community manager is the right corporate response. You won't see that very often on Toyota's fan page. Where's the engagement? The top-down approach lives.

Conversely, check out Audi's Facebook page. It responds to negative comments and interacts with friends throughout the week and the weekend. Its conversational tone is superior to that of the other auto manufacturers, who seem to either boast too much or use flat, corporate tones.

For a nonprofit perspective, go to a well-run Facebook fan page like the Humane Society of the United States, and you'll see three times the interaction from a community manager than you would on most nonprofit sites. This is participation-based communications. It's real, it's human and it's the kind of dialogue that people crave from companies. As powerful as these two brands are in their own fields, they don't take an above-the-masses attitude.

Why does this work? Because companies are made of

people, and people want to talk to people, not brands. Over
and over again, we've seen this approach work, from Zappos
and Comcast Cares to LIVESTRONG and the National Wildlife
Federation.

To become well liked by the Fifth Estate, you must become
a member of the Fifth Estate. Consider the difference. The
traditional method has your spokespeople — in the modern
parlance, community managers — talking from ivory towers
delivering messages. But in most social communities this is
considered spamming. You need to get out there and have real
dialogue with people.[72]

Consider the Altimeter Group's recent study, "The 8 Success Criteria For Facebook Page Marketing."[73] Three of these
marketing recommendations hold key tenants here. Be Up to
Date" suggests an 80/20 rule, where only 20 percent of your
updates are about the company or organization. "Live Authenticity" and "Participate in Dialog" encourage organizations to
provide a real person who has genuine, two-way conversations
with people in real time, not someone delivering messaging.

From a social media standpoint, this means transforming
the top-down marketing of information into a more , factual,
journalistic approach. You're an expert in your subject matter
— so give them your information in a way that is responsive
to community comments and concerns. This is what the community values, wants and needs, though it's not necessarily
what the organization wants to promote.

Will it hurt your communications? No! Believe it or not,
even when providing factual information, everyone assumes
the organization is biased. There's really little need to twist
arms; people assume you want to sell products or advance

your cause. In fact, a smart, integrated approach will have calls to action to do just those things.

When it comes to the actual social part of the equation, focus on building relationships through good information and conversation to foster goodwill between you and the public, the community, employees and customers. This is the role of a modern ombudsmen representing an organization, the attitude of a Fifth Estate member who wishes to become an integral part of the community.

Moving from Silos to Hives

Revolutions involve violent, sudden change. Evolution dictates a migratory path toward change. While many Fifth Estate members cry for a revolution from the organizations that serve them, social media should instead approach the current culture in an evolutionary fashion. Social media won't be accepted by an organization if it is a sudden uprising. Migration offers the best path to change.

Communication at its core is the exchange of thoughts, opinions or information by oral, written or visual means. It is more than just marketing, and by tracking the information flow, you can see its organizational architecture, workflow and cultural values.

Let's consider a beehive for a moment. The basic nest architecture for all honey bees is similar: "Honey is stored in the upper part of the comb; beneath it are rows of pollen-storage cells, worker-brood cells, and drone-brood cells, in that order. The peanut-shaped queen cells are normally built at the lower edge of the comb."[74]

Hives are adjacent to each other, and while their members all have roles, from producers (honey) and defenders to mates and rulers, these hives allow for fluid interaction. This is a much different mindset than a traditional corporate architecture of silos. Silos or traditional departments are often represented as stand alone boxes connected by lines in the traditional organizational chart. Hive architecture allows for fluid information transfer and interaction among roles with hive cells placed next to each other on each independent face, as well as creating more open access to the outside.

Social media eases the process of moving toward an extended corporate hive with more empowered departments that an engage with outside world more frequently. A new structure embracing social media means empowering internal and external stakeholders with the ability to communicate, work and share information more fluidly across extended architecture.

Social media is not meant to gut the organization or its purpose. Instead it should support a better outcome by helping the culture migrate to modern information use. The results can be more productivity, better customer relationships, financial rewards and better, revamped policies.

Evolving Processes and Policy

To successfully adapt, executives should examine department, division and enterprise missions and explore natural directions for improvement. This leads to a measurable social media result. Time management, improved processes, outbound marketing communications, better customer relations, product marketing/development, return on investment or other organizational improvements are all achievable goals.

Marketing is the most talked-about mechanism, but there are

others—including customer service, investor relations and human resources. Whether it's ensuring message integrity in conversation, publishing public statements (and associated processes), handling legal issues or measuring performance, many processes within an enterprise stop people from using social media tools. I know of one consultancy that tells its staff to use social media, but then asks workers why their billable time is down.

Adapt your HR and workflow processes to enable social media participation, instead of punishing people for it. Let people use the tools to talk to each other. Lower the firewall enough to let external stakeholders participate.

Old industrial processes seek to close silos in an effort to compete and protect. Those defense mechanisms don't always work anymore. Each process should be vetted in light of the potential gain. Does the risk this seeks to avoid really outweigh what we can achieve? Adjust accordingly. Here are some examples:

• Is there a process to vet online customer feedback? Or does the customer service department not interact with communications? And why?

• Review processes that involve many stakeholders across the organization. Taking weeks to approve a news release or a Web page will not allow for live conversations about real issues

• Set aside the notion that you will stick to a prescribed plan or course of action. Planning campaigns assumes that you are calling the shots. The new online communications environment is so fluid that more effective communicators have a playbook, and they enable rapid adjustment to the evolving conversations that arise with the Fifth Estate. Often, substitutions are needed, and new paths develop.

• Impressions (clicks) and page views are no longer viable measurement.

• Interactions with the Fifth Estate that lead toward a goal are. How are people rewarded for successfully communicating and participating?

• In that vein, if 30 percent of your stakeholders' time is spent online, have performance and job review measurements been adjusted to reflect that 30 percent online work? Or are people only going to get promoted for the number of media hits, trade show leads or webinar registrants?

• Does your legal department prevent communication from occurring? And is that protection worth it in the new environment?

It's all about empowering the front line that interacts with the Fifth Estate and associated stakeholders; more people power versus less control.

Don't relinquish quality checks. The reality is while more brainpower is good; there are still dangers to crowdsourcing and idea markets. They require a lot of community management, process and strategic direction (More on crowdsourcing in Chapters 4 and 7).[75]

At their core, beehives still have queens. And organizations—while evolving to become Fifth Estate members with more open, information-friendly architectures—still need management and direction. Great decision making, while informed by additional and more varied sources, still runs companies. Intelligently vetting information sources becomes a crucial component of making strong decisions.

Case Study: American Red Cross Crisis Data

During any crisis, the American Red Cross, response agencies and government organizations receive hundreds—even thousands—of reports and requests for help from social media users. These calls for help are not always answered. Reports range from detailed analysis filed from a computer to text messages from smartphone users.

A survey conducted by the American Red Cross showed that 69 percent of Americans said that emergency responders should be monitoring social media sites in order to quickly send help—and nearly half believe a response agency is probably already responding to any urgent request they might see. Moreover, 74 percent expected help to come less than an hour after their tweet or Facebook post.

Currently there is no process or technology identified to facilitate sharing and validating this data, although tools like Ushahidi are starting to make strides. Routing these social media reports would be a crucial next step in crisis response for governing agencies. The American Red Cross wanted to take the lead in starting a conversation to consider next-generation social networking tools to extend its capacity to facilitate crisis response to the larger community.

Engagement

The capacity to respond could be developed from three camps: tech-savvy community of providers and agencies, from first responders and government, and from the wider community of social media users. The American Red Cross wanted to resolve how to effectively collaborate with these groups to manage expectations and make progress toward a solution. On a second level, the power of the community to help each other during a crisis is largely untapped and could

---

potentially fuel the relevance of the Red Cross for years to come. In the words of Wendy Harman, "Your neighbors are your first responders."

The American Red Cross began by defining the problem to key stakeholders. A whitepaper was publicized on a Posterous Blog (http://emergencysocialdata.posterous.com/) that gave compelling examples from prior disasters to demonstrate severity, outline the survey results, and develop a list of questions to be addressed at the Emergency Social Data Summit. All materials and event promotions were made available on a unified page at the American Red Cross blog (http://redcrosschat.org/about-the-emergency-social-data-summit).

The Emergency Social Data White Paper and the survey findings were provided to both influencers online as well as the traditional media. the American Red Cross's well-followed Twitter and Facebook accounts were used to announce the availability of these materials. They also heavily promoted these materials to the attendees, who were encouraged to use the Twitter hashtagged, "#crisisdata" in their online conversations.

The Red Cross developed the content and promoted a summit, which was held simultaneously at Red Cross headquarters in Washington, D.C., and online on Aug. 12, 2010. The event was attended in person by approximately 160 high-level government, media, social media, tech, nonprofit organizations and local responders. Online participation occurred using social media via hashtags, U-Stream, and a Twitter-specific chat with more than 1,000 participants The off- and online real-time feedback and participation was recorded in a crisis data wiki.

The effort was wrapped with a summary report from the conference with findings, suggestions and challenges moving forward. This document synthesized the main ideas from the event and the live town hall. It included recommendations for vetting technology ideas, including seven areas for the community to focus to build a next-generation emergency social data response system.

Results

The American Red Cross received input from a wide variety of sources that will help shape the nonprofit's future efforts. By the numbers:

1. The white paper was read 878 times as of Aug. 24, 2010 (Scrib'd data).

2. 167 people attended the Emergency Social Data Summit in Washington, D.C., on Aug. 12, 2010. Attendees included first responders, local and federal government, media and citizens and technology companies. High-level influencers attended and participated in the conference, including the White House, FEMA, CNN, several influential bloggers and many others (see full speakers list http://bit.ly/bwax53).

3. On Aug. 12, 2010, 4,730 tweets with the hashtag #crisisdata were sent. For an eight-day period, Aug. 10-17, 2010, there were 5,742 tweets from 1,267 contributors, exceeding 1,000 online participants.

4. On Twitter, more than 50 percent of the tweets were retweets, showing that the nuggets being shared were viral and being shared widely.

5. 396 people registered to watch the online event via UStream, and on average there were about 300 people watching the stream during the event.

6. 385 mentions across blogs and Facebook demonstrated a larger conversation occurring about the topic, inspired by the conference itself, its marketing, the study or associated news coverage.

7. The #crisisdata hashtag (wthashtag.com/Crisisdata) is being used 50-100 times a week after the conference to continue the conversation and share research and documentation to further this cause.

The Red Cross is now in conversations with several organizations and programs to address these issues. In addition, working groups (which are outlined in the final chapter of the white paper) will be convening over the coming months to work out details for possible solutions to better address crisis data.

The Role of Social Media Policy

The organizational social media policy becomes a crucial document for employees. It defines what is safe to do, what the organization frowns upon and how employees can navigate their day-to-day responsibilities while maintaining a social presence.

A social media policy is a living document reflecting management's ethos about how much latitude the organization allows in online public conversations. As an organization becomes comfortable with social media and its interactions with the Fifth Estate, the policy likely will encourage more transparency and authenticity. It also will reflect lessons learned: some of them are painful but necessary experiences on the path toward more extended, networked communications.

Several best-practices documents have been created on what should be included in such a policy. Consider recommendations by Cision (http://bit.ly/cisionSMP) and the Society of New Communications Research (SNCR) (http://bit.ly/SNCRSMP). These are good starting points, but keep in mind that your culture is unique. You may have special qualities to showcase or regulations that prevent you from talking openly (SEC, HIPPA, government clearance, client/case confidentiality). Perhaps your organization just wants to be conservative with its initial use of social media, and that's okay, too.

The Social Media Governance site published a list of open social media policies (http://bit.ly/SMgovern) representing almost every type of organization imaginable, from Cisco to the New Zealand State Services Commission.[76] Your organization might want to review them to see which ones work for you and your type of business or nonprofit. You could find that parts of different policies fit your organization. Feel free to use them, as long as you provide attribution, as the American Red Cross did with its social media policy for personal communications.[77]

Just remember that many of your employees are members of the Fifth Estate themselves. To deny access in any form only encourages anonymous postings and veiled remarks. After all, to become truly visible in social media, you must, at least to some extent, participate in the Fifth Estate as a community member.[78]

CHAPTER THREE SNAPSHOTS

To effectively communicate with members of the Fifth Estate, organizations need to transform their cultures to enable success. Most organizations are structured to compete in a mass communications world, but within micromedia forms, those cultures are antiquated. The process of looking inside and adapting an organization's culture is a crucial precursor to social media success.

Culture and Silos

When faced with a new technology or function, most organizations delegate its use to a specific department, effectively creating a silo of expertise. However, silos prevent free-flowing, networked communications and hurt social media adoption. The top five silos in a company are executive management, communications, IT, sales and marketing, and legal.

Executives and Communicators Lead the Change

Change within an organization starts at the top. Without executives leading the charge, it's unlikely that an organization will adopt social media successfully. Similarly, communicators provide a key adoption point. When they move to embrace conversations as opposed to trying to control them, they become a key ingredient of social media success.

Moving from Silos to Hives: Examining Processes

Once the organizational drivers are in place, transformation can begin. This change is evolutionary, not revolutionary. Processes should be examined in a manner that facilitates information flow. One way to visualize a process is to consider whether or not it allows for networked interactions, similar to a beehive. This allows for hierarchy, while empowering individuals.

The Role of Social Media Policy

A social media policy helps you communicate your organization's approach to online communication for employees. It helps adoption and facilitates clear understanding of what can and cannot be done. This living document should reflects the organization's evolving experience.

Chapter 4
Crafting a Strategy

You've invested a lot of time and effort to connect with the Fifth Estate. Now it's time to build your communications strategy for online media. Traditionally, when engaging in a marketing effort, organizations establish a goal or desired outcome, identify their target audiences and map their strategies. Acting much like a general in the field, the most successful communicators research their audience before they engage, understanding their stakeholders' needs. Then they ascertain which media to use, what timing to employ, how to use tactics within those media and implement calls to action they must use to achieve their goals. The strategists often select the tactics most likely to succeed within their budget, create measurements to guage the success of their efforts and, finally, launch their campaign.

Social media and technical savvy do not equate to marketing strategy.[79] Nor do blogs, a bookmarking widget or crowdsourcing. What does count is creating a meaningful way, a method, an overarching course, to attract and keep the attention of your stakeholders. The rest is tactical.

Some say that social media does not deserve a strategy, that it is a tactical tool set. Others disagree. In reality, it's neither. You can have strategy with social media, with integrated communications or with traditional communications alone. The definition of strategy remains simple. According to the Oxford Dictionary, it is "a plan of action or policy designed to achieve a major or overall aim." As communicators, we overcomplicate the conversation about plans to get from A to B with discussions about tactics. It is no coincidence that many communications "strategies," with or without social media, often are really justifications for communications program existence or merely tactics in disguise. Other plans have an overabundance of tactics, ways for organizations to play with the latest shiny social media tools. These "strategies" lack the context of a plan to achieve an objective.

The Fifth Estate can use social media to talk back and even to reject online communications. It also can use it to reject traditional communications. In late 2008, Motrin launched an ad campaign on a Friday targeted toward mothers with young children. The ad intimated that back pain caused by carrying a child would cause mothers to cry, and that Motrin was there for them. Bloggers who were moms found the ad patronizing and started tweeting and blogging about it. Motrin wasn't listening. By the weekend's end, the Motrin brand was in the middle of a firestorm that ended up taking a week to subside. And it took a public apology from Motrin and parent company Johnson & Johnson, which pulled the advertisement.

Social media's inherently two-way nature creates a tool set that requires unique approaches and subsets of strategy to successfully engage the Fifth Estate. Further, many communications departments try to ignore social voices, as was the case with Motrin. Mistake. As we have seen over and over, the Fourth and Fifth Estates are intrinsically linked. While you may have a unique social media strategy, it would be unwise to keep it isolated within the organization because your traditional media relations, customer service and donor relations all may be affected in short order. [80]

When it's well-integrated, the whole communications effort is better—in large part because the Fifth Estate members don't delineate and parse the types of media they consume into boxes like social, broadcast, print and cable. You would be hard-pressed to find someone who literally says to their friends, "I am going to use social media tonight." (Integration is discussed in Chapter 5 as part of tactical execution.) Most people go about their day inundated by a variety of media and messages, and they rarely can remember where they first saw a brand or product. Communicators are in a perpetual losing battle for the attention of media-saturated minds, and that's why strategy matters now more than ever.[81] A well-devised strategy enables your program to break through the clutter. The truth is, advertising (and more recently, media relations) started to lose effectiveness a long time ago. This diminution led to Positioning theories and strategies from Al Ries and Jack Trout 30 years ago.[82] At that time, there were only 50 cable channels and no consumer Internet, much less social media. The situation since has grown much more ominous for communicators as their empty platitudes and PR messages fall flat, failing at astonishing rates.

At the heart of Positioning was an understanding of what makes people fall in love with causes, products, services and ideas. Getting into the minds of donors, advocates, citizens and buyers, and enticing them to become interested in your efforts is a great accomplishment. It's hard cutting through the clutter, achieving impact and retaining their commitment. It means you've listened, that you understand them, value them, and can build meaningful experiences that resonate in their minds and hearts. You have cultivated the trust of the Fifth Estate and positioned yourself to cut through the extremely fractured traditional and social media environment. You will not only be heard, but possibly even welcomed. In this media environment, that's a form of seduction. And it's also a sign of a good old-fashioned marketing strategy.[83]

Positioning has been important in two-party engagements for millennia. Consider Sun Tzu's classic quote from the ancient Chinese military text *Art of War*, "The art of war teaches us to rely not on the likelihood of the enemy's not coming, but on our own readiness to receive him; not on the chance of his not attacking, but rather on the fact that we have made our position unassailable."[84] True, your chosen community is not your enemy, but they are also not your willing cohort in marketing. It is important to consider your effort from their point of view, and that's why great campaigns find their basis in strategic positioning statements.

Your positioning statement should dictate the messages used during media interactions. If your cause, service or product is worthy and you are successfully positioned, communicating becomes easy. In social media, as with advertising, if you can create meaningful communications, then your strategy is likely to work across diverse traditional media, as well. The only thing that changes are the tactics. Positioning is all about finding a way to cut through the clutter with a strategy that sets you apart and persuades stakeholders that they should give you that listen.

Great strategies are unique and simple, and they ring clear and true. They stand out in a crowd and attract the right people—those whose attention we are working so hard to attain. But as the author of *Made to Stick*, Dan Heath, said, "Simple is not easy."[85] The simpler a plan is, the more elegant it is.

Consider the name of a social media darling charity: water. Right away people assume the cause is water related, an accurate depiction of the 501(c)(3) that seeks to provide clean water in African countries. Successful simplicity requires a deft hand. It is the mark of the truly experienced craftsman. People should be proud to be simple.

A community's interests lie at the heart of any social media initiative. Initiatives succeed when an organization creates content that serves those interests.[86]

If you have read this book to this point, then you already are listening to your online community to get an understanding of your stakeholders. So keep it simple. If you know your community is 50 rocket scientists in the western United States, create your initiative for them, not the entire blogosphere. Whether they are affiliated en masse with a community like Facebook or a micro-community of philatelists who use blogs to discuss their latest stamp finds, your stakeholders enjoy specific types of information and content that is relevant to them.

It's important to explore your competitors and their initiatives. Are they respected by the community? Are they being discussed—negatively or positively? See how the community reacts to organizations selling to them versus organizations successfully turning the community into advocates for their services. Analyze their efforts in comparison to your research findings about what makes the community tick. Some of these efforts will have failed, and it's important to know why.

In some cases, you can use market research studies—surveys of social network members. Some networks like Facebook and LinkedIn offer these direct-access forms of research.[87] Many members will not take the survey, but that is similar to survey participation in the brick–and–mortar world.

Your existing listening program, your initial efforts at social media within your organization, and your analysis of the competitive space and any market research available should make it possible to map out a successful social media program. Look for pointers, including specific subject areas, types of popular stories, and content and noted hot topics.

If strategy can be defined as the terms and conditions of how to engage with the Fifth Estate (or whether to engage at all), then there are many unique ways to do so. Individual voices, teams, mainstream social networks, applications, pages, groups, documents, wikis, your blog, their blogs—the list goes on and on. Be careful. In a world full of bells and whistles it's easy to succumb to "shiny-object syndrome." Instead, it's important focus on the actual strategy, the plan of approach toward your community.

The following four categories are the primary types of social media strategy that organizations use online:

Participation: This may refer to an individual (often called a social media or community manager) or, in more sophisticated organizations, a team of people whose job is to have conversations with their communities of interest. The primary purposes of their activity are interaction, building trust and developing relationships. Most customer service accounts on Twitter fall into this category.

Participation also is a precursor for success in the other three primary areas of social media strategy. In many ways it's a two-step of listening and responding—basic, functional and necessary for any kind of dance, and utilitarian enough that you can get away with it for one night. In addition, participation is a maintenance strategy to continue a presence between large initiatives.

One of the best examples of an organization that fosters participation is the nonprofit Social Media Club. It's no coincidence that co-founder Chris Heuer is one of the original proponents of participation marketing on the social web. Social Media Club began in 2006 with meetings in San Francisco. Now more than 200 chapters exist around the globe to host conversations on and offline that explore key societal issues raised by transformative social technologies.

Service: Want to make Fifth Estate friends? Serve it with great data, content and applications. This seems pretty easy, but there's a fine line between serving and spamming that most inexperienced marketers don't recognize. In fact, many organizations begin their social media experiences by publishing content without knowing what their audience is, or if they even have one.

If you engage in listening as the necessary precursor to social media engagement, your success becomes much likelier. Add participation and network-building before serving the community with content, and your chance of success increases further. Your application, wiki or content will be much more likely to resonate with the community, because your organization will be better informed about what it wants.

An example of a content server is Rubbermaid, with its Adventures in Organization blog. Some entries feature products, but in all cases the blog explains about how to organize your house, other places or when on outings. "Adventures in Organization" provides potential stakeholders with practical information that matters in their day-to-day lives.[88]

Top-Down: Many organizations assume they will not be able to invest the time in the grassroots effort necessary for full community participation, nor do they want to commit to a long-term content offering. Instead, they opt to build relationships with influencers, people that the larger community trusts and responds to, from bloggers to active social network participants. They seek blog coverage or social network profile endorsements, using a relevant offering to the influencer. By building relationships with critical influencers, they hope the communities that follow those leading voices will follow suit.

The Gap engaged in an outreach program before the 2010 BlogHer conference, offering 100 influential female bloggers a $400 shopping allowance and a styling appointment at a local Gap. These women were described as influencers and speakers at a conference where Gap clothes would be seen by hundreds of other women. Many speakers tweeted using a #gapmagic hashtag and blogged about their experience, and most wore their new Gap clothes during the conference. "Smart marketing all around," Marketing Roadmaps blogger and Gap Magic participant Susan Getgood said.[89]

Empowerment: The hardest of all forms of social media strategy, empowerment assumes that the organization will commit to building a far-flung community. The empowered Fifth Estate members create conversations and ideas that are so extensive they exist well beyond the organization's reach. Instead, the company or nonprofit becomes much more of a host and facilitator, available when called upon. The organization then creates initiatives and helps to sustain the effort over the long term. Crowdsourcing—including large-scale multi-city events, cause-based initiatives and far-flung internal organizational communities—is the most common example of the empowerment strategy.

Consider 350's efforts with this type of strategy. The nonprofit organizes an annual global day of environmental action to reduce carbon dioxide omissions. 350 uses social tools to help local organizers develop their own events, to promote the events and to keep their stakeholders informed. In 2010, 350 is organizied 10/10/10 Work Parties to get people focused on actions, signing up more than ,000 event organizers in 188 countries,

Most individual strategies fall under one of those four classifications. More than one strategy type can be in play at once, obviously, depending on an organization's capacity and initiative.

We will examine each of these four types of social media

strategy in more depth. But first, we need to explore and explain Shiny Object Syndrome.

Shiny Object Syndrome: Don't Fondle the Hammer

When seeking to inspire a conversation about one's initiative—whether it's a product, a cause or simply education—the first instinct is to reach for the hot, shiny tool of the day. Since *Now Is Gone* was written, the shine has shifted from blogs to Facebook/Twitter, then to widgets and applications, then to iPhone and Android apps, then to location–based networks that let you check into places and post comments on your phone like FourSquare and Gowalla, then to tablets like the iPad and so on.

First dubbed "Shiny Object Syndrome" by PR–Squared bnlogger Todd Defren in 2005, this phenomenon drives organizations, companies and individuals to adapt the hottest new social communications tool, often[90] based on peer pressure, buzz or a desire to be one of the first. The syndrome undercuts strategic approaches to social media communication.

Ace social technology analyst Jeremiah Owyang has called the phenomenon "Fondling the Hammer"[91] because Web strategists often focus on the tool rather than on their approach. While we have a general strategy toward creating a great conversation, we need to best understand how to participate within that community and create an approach that will work with it, rather than just running to the shelf and picking up the latest cool tool.

Shiny Object Syndrome can waste financial resources, resulting in terrible consequences for organizations, executives and communicators alike.

In Charlene Li and Josh Bernoff's classic book *Ground-swell*, the statement "concentrate on the relationships, not the technologies Is almost perfect. The community drives social media. The technology does not drive the Fifth Estate, but rather empowers it with a continually evolving set of tools. Li and Bernoff also note that Shiny Object Syndrome can become a major barrier to success.[92]

Getting beyond a focus on tools requires the lead communicator to revisit the master conversation strategy.[93] As unsexy as it is, a blog or a widget may still be your most powerful tool. A healthy evaluation of social media tools should reveal which ones your stakeholders and their influencers are using—and thus which you should use as you seek to forge relationships with them.

Participation is Marketing

Participation means more than simply acting as a member of the Fifth Estate. It means contributing to its success. Go beyond simply talking ton build value for a community. While dialogue is definitely a big part of an organization's role in this new world, it's still crucial to do more. Comment on other relevant sites, discuss issues that matter to the larger community (and not just your organization's business), link back to other sites and participate in the community's relevant events.

There are many ways to take part, and many contemporary marketing blogs and books discuss these specific tactics. But there's still a strategic approach to participation that many marketers fail to recognize.

Social Media Club co-founder Chris Heuer emphasizes that participation equates to direct marketing in online social networks. It's at this basic point that the concept of an organization as a member of the community occurs.[94]

Heuer said: "The reason for [an organization's] formation was to help people with a specific problem, desire or need—that the all-important intention of contributing to the community by participating in it was their original purpose. It is this key shift in thinking, returning to the roots of our society and the organization's role in it, that is represented by my simple, snack-sized sound bite that participation is marketing."[95]

Through participation, your organization builds great relationships, you will encourage your community members to tell you what they need, and your business will thrive because it's helping people. In short, participation attracts customers from your specific community. These customers build more value through relationship-oriented loyalty as opposed to simply being satisfied with a purchase or experience.[96] This is true of small and large organizations.

LIVESTRONG has a high interaction rate with its Facebook fans, Twitter followers and on its blog. The conversational tone is one of camaraderie, and it extends beyond the official page and handle and into the staff's communications online. LIVESTRONG CEO Doug Ulman leads the charge, while Brooke McMillan, the community manager, maintains a steady presence.

Case Study: Network Solutions
"Voice of the Customer" Program

Network Solutions sought to engage in a reputation building social public relations effort called Voice of the

Customer. Phase one began on July 1, 2008, as an effort to directly engage generators of negative commentary on blogs, Twitter and forums in a listen-and-respond conversation. The company was receiving 58 percent negative comments on blog posts, comments and social network posts (as of June 30, 2008). This was caused by a variety of issues, from its own service to negative coverage from prominent such Fifth Estate bloggers as Michael Arrington.

The goal of the program was to reduce negative commentary by more than 20 percent, effectively positioning the company as a more reputable solutions provider. At the heart of the reputation-management program was a serious, long-term commitment from Network Solutions to identify, listen to and attempt to promptly resolve problems. The company believed just saying "we care" wasn't enough, and it sought to do everything possible to resolve problems. It used the Voice of the Customer as a catalyst to evolve Network Solutions offerings.

Engagement

Network Solutions' effort started behind Director of Social Media Shashi Bellamkonda's considerable Twitter presence, a new customer-service-oriented Twitter account called @netsolcares to resolve negative tweets and a blog called "Solutions Are Power." In addition, a listening program was deployed so that Network Solutions could participate in negative conversations about the company, and thus hopefully resolve issues.

In some cases, Network Solutions couldn't provide the answer people wanted to hear, but people knew the company was engaged. It made an immediate difference. Consider the following commentary:

Maybe this Social Media Thing Works After All: "It takes a certain level of complete and utter dissatisfaction for someone (or at least me) to blog about it. It's unfortunate that a blog entry (NOT our letter to customer service) caught the attention of the uppers at Network Solutions, but it's smart of them to monitor the chatter. And it's appreciated, as a person who had a situation that needed rectifying."

The company noticed an immediate downtick in negative comments and a surprisingly warm embrace of the company's efforts. Emboldened, the company began diversifying its efforts based on feedback over months and eventually years. It launched a study and an associated conference to serve small business owners with pertinent information about growing a business online. It added a content channel—Women Grow Business.

"Just by beginning a conversation, Network Solutions was able to show its customers that it cared for feedback and was willing to assist existing customers and prospects," Bellamkonda said. "Through the GrowSmartBiz conference and events for entrepreneurs and small business, Network Solutions showed thought leadership that the community appreciated with positive blog posts."

Results

Network Solutions reduced negative commentary about the company from 58 percent to 23 percent. Even more importantly, positive conversations online significantly increased, from 20 percent to 54 percent, helping the company develop a new, more positive reputation in social media circles. Given that it's an Internet services company, this was a primary influencer audience for the organization.

Today, Network Solutions may have as many as 2,500 customer engagements a month on Twitter. On Facebook, 50 percent of Network Solutions' group actively engages with the company for customer service, active discussions. Finally, while the company sought to manage its reputation through social media, it can attribute approximately $400,000 of direct revenue to social media efforts.

Intangible benefits include a shift in perception of Network Solutions as not just a domain registrar but also a thought leader in small business growth. The company is often cited for its ability to use social media tools to maximize its customers' satisfaction. Finally, Network Solutions won the 2008 SNCR Award for Excellence in Corporate Reputation Management using Social Media and the 2009 Golden Quill Award for Excellence in Social Media.

The Editorial Mission: Build Value for the Community

The pyramid below demonstrates the service-oriented model, using the technographics profile created by Charlene Li and Josh Bernoff to explain the types of Fifth Estate members. From this perspective, the organizational social communicator uses social media tools to create valuable content, ultimately meant to serve spectators—specifically, an organization's stakeholders. In this model, basic Fifth Estate members have the power to participate (or not), and as such they should be kept on top or given the most power in the overall community by joining the conversation through friending or subscription, collecting by creating bookmarks or sharing links, or criticizing with direct interaction. Any member of the Fifth Estate also can be a content creator, as the ladder is fluid. (Find out what your community's technographic profile is here: http://bit.ly/seeyours.)

Content and social media marketing is best approached in this way—as opposed to top–down. Serving the community becomes the top priority[97],and creating value builds opportunity in a win-win fashion for your organization and for your larger community. In this particular instance, valuable

Service-Oriented Conversation Pyramid

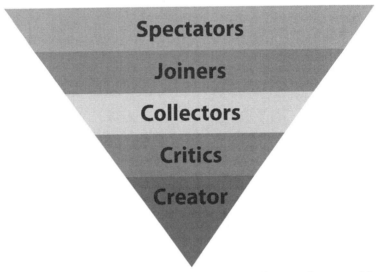

and well-structured content geared toward a social network's needs allows you to contribute, participate and also garner respect. By creating content and tools that better suit the Fifth Estate's needs, its members will naturally come to trust your effort and will want to communicate with you.

It may seem parochial, but one thing organizational Fifth Estate media creators can learn from the Fourth Estate is the creation of exceptional content aimed at a particular community. Garnering thousands, or millions, of readers (depending on the size of the community) requires superior content, continued innovation and ongoing creativity.

"In order to implement a successful strategy, think like a publisher," said David Meerman Scott in his book, *The New*

Rules of Marketing & PR. "Marketers at the organizations successfully using the new rules recognize the fact that they are not purveyors of information, and they manage content as a valuable asset with the same care that a publishing company does."[98]

Great social media efforts use an editorial mission to guide content creation and fulfill a purpose. One of the most popular sites on the Internet, Lolcats from ICanHazCheezburger, features user-generated content with cats caught in unusual positions and fanciful captions written by their owners. Though there is a less-popular dog version, you will not see dog pictures on Lolcats, nor will you see hamsters. Its singular focus makes the site a big success. It also has extended the content to become a successful iPhone application.

In traditional media, on–target content is written with a purpose to educate or inform readers, listeners or viewers about a particular or general subject matter. If content wavers from that mission, a managing or executive editor whose job centers on fulfilling the editorial objective and serving the community often discards it.

Marketers have to understand the importance of editorial missions—not only for outbound PR efforts, but for their own online media efforts. By sticking to an editorial mission statement, your media—applications, blogs, widgets or pages —stay on track, creating value for the community by providing relevant content and tools.

There's a major pitfall to avoid in an editorial mission: overtly promoting the company. This error still is one of the most common reasons organizational media initiatives fail. Communicators engage in social media because they want to market themselves, and they think social media forms are just another way to promote their wares. This error creates applications, blogs, Facebook pages, Twitter feeds, videos and widgets that are never downloaded, played, read or used.

Promotional content and applications bore the casual Fifth Estate member. People don't care about organizations unless they better their lives. Consider a recent Pew Internet study that shows people's primary reason for interacting online. Eighty-five percent of Americans agreed with this statement: "In 2010, when I look at the big picture and consider my personal friendships, marriage and other relationships, I see that the Internet has mostly been a positive force on my social world."[99] Become a positive force in your stakeholders' world with your content, and you will succeed.

Sales pitches have no inherent value to someone who's interested in the company's general category. Simply being sold to by a corporation fails to meet casual users' needs and defeats the reason behind their use of social media. Content must appeal to the community, and this means making it valuable and interesting. Promotion only works when it creates substantial value for your community.

Content should be authentic, providing information consistent with the organization's natural areas of expertise. This expertise is the organization's primary source of value to a community. Further, sharing relevant, interesting, subject-matter-specific content allows the company to build its image as a community leader and expert.

Though an editorial mission may change as your media initiative evolves, the mission shapes your creation of content, ensuring that it stays on track.

Also important are editorial standards that give general guidance for content creation. For example, encourage cross-linking and references to other blogs, avoid attacks on others and limit videos to two minutes. These are guidelines that help your effort become consistent and known to its community. Of course, guidelines should be flexible, but content can wander without them.

Case Study: InvisiblePeople.TV

Mark Horvath is a free agent, a one-man army who has taken social media tools to fight homelessness as a video blogger, and now, because of his efforts, he has evolved his efforts to become a 501c3 certified charity. What started and continues as InvisiblePeople.tv has recently evolved to include We Are Visible (wearevisible.com), a site that provides homeless people with online tools to communicate, connect, tell their stories and engage in action.

InvisiblePeople.tv wants to change the general public's paradigms on homelessness. Basically, it empowers homeless people to tell their own stories using YouTube, Twitter and InvisiblePeople.tv. The strategy revolves around content through good storytelling and providing real tangible actions, a participation ethos of treating everyone with respect, doing what is right even when others don't, and gratitude.

"The goal is to make the 'invisible people' in society more visible by bringing them out of the shadows where they are ignored," Horvath said. "We're using social media to expose the pain, hardship and hopelessness that millions of people face each day."

Engagement

Since its launch in November 2008, InvisiblePeople.tv has used video blog (vlog) entries and social networks to share the compelling, gritty and unfiltered stories of homeless people from Los Angeles to Washington, D.C. The vlog gets up close and personal with veterans, mothers, children, layoff victims and others who have been forced onto the streets by a variety of circumstances.

Each week, Horvath highlights homeless citizens' stories on InvisiblePeople.tv and high-traffic sites such as YouTube, Twitter and Facebook, proving to a global audience that while the homeless often may be ignored, they are far from invisible. One story at a time, videos posted on InvisiblePeople.tv deliver a call to action that is being answered by national brands, nonprofit organizations and everyday citizens who now are committed to participating in the fight against homelessness. In addition, founder Mark Horvath is an outstanding networker at conferences and online, cultivating strong relationships with crucial influencers across the blogosphere.

At the time of writing, Horvath had just launched We Are Visible, which provides people dealing with poverty and homelessness the tools they need to get online and have a voice. The site teaches them how to sign up for e-mail, open a Twitter account, join Facebook, create a blog and, in general, take advantage of the benefits of online social media. It also has the potential to become a model for virtual case management as it helps build a community among homeless people and support-service providers.

Results

Horvath would tell you that hits, page views and followers probably all are important. But the real results happen when people take action. Here are some of the many actions Horvath has inspired:

- Getting a homeless veteran's RV out of impound.
- Starting housing programs.
- Providing shelter for homeless citizens.
- Providing homeless children with new shoes.
- A farmer donated 40 acres of land that is now being

farmed to grow food for low income families at a public school.

- Providing a homeless citizen with a tablet to blog.
- Providing shelter and gifts to a homeless family during Christmas.

"There are far too many things to list," Horvath said. "YouTube gave us the front page for 24 hours, and over 2 million people touched homelessness who would have probably rolled up their window at an exit ramp.

"The cool thing about We Are Visible is that homeless people are helping other homeless people," Horvath added. "I didn't expect that. One homeless father is even collecting cans to print We Are Visible fliers to hand out."

The History of Influencer Theory

Successful online word-of-mouth or grassroots marketing involves an attention phase where community influencers embrace and spread the message. Many organizations who do not have the resources or the time to allocate to a long-term participation or content initiative opt to engage in influencer relations. They add blogger and social network influencer lists to their media relations pitch sheet. But while assigning Fifth Estate relations to people who normally interact with the Fourth Estate may make linear sense, it contradicts the nature of the social web and the way it works. Online communities are about participation, and media relations tends to revolve around pitching people story ideas, similar to sales.

In fact, the dynamics of influence is a highly disputed topic, and getting your idea embraced by those who can best spread the word could require a different strategy than simply purchasing a list. The discussion about what influence really is has been ongoing since the social web first began.

Nine years ago, Malcolm Gladwell's *The Tipping Point* (2002) discussed influencers by describing Connectors, Mavens and Salesmen models. Gladwell argued that select sets of people disseminate ideas to the public, and they have unique attributes—trust networks, subject-matter expertise or sales skills.

Yahoo's Duncan Watts wrote a widely discussed counterpoint to Gladwell on Fast Company a couple of years ago dismissing "The Law of the Few":

...in the large majority of cases, the cascade began with an average Joe (although in cases where an Influential touched off the trend, it spread much further). To stack the deck in favor of Influentials, Watts changed the simulation, making them 10 times more connected... But the rank-and-file citizen was still far more likely to start a contagion.[100]

Other important books have discussed the influencers, and in particular their online role. They augment the power of the few theory:

• Ben McConnell and Jackie Huba's book *Citizen Marketers* (2006) discusses the one-percenters, the select few content creators who drive online conversations.

• Chris Brogan and Julien Smith discussed influencers' role in social media in *Trust Agents* (2009). Their theory centers on building online trust and relationships rather than marketing messages to drive influence.

• Beth Kanter and Allison Fine's *The Networked Nonprofit* (2010) features uber-influential free agents crashing into the walls of storied cultures.

There are those who swear influencers can be limited to a much smaller group known as Dunbar's number—roughly

150 people (the concept was first proposed by British anthropologist Robin Dunbar). Dunbar's theory acknowledges a cognitive limit to the number of people with whom one can maintain stable social relationships. These are relationships in which an individual knows who each person is and how each person relates to every other person.[101]

So which theory is correct? Where's the influence—with the uber-connected one-percenter as discussed by Jackie Huba, or the Kanter/Fine free agent? Or the person who lights the spark within his/her community of 150? Well, all are right and wrong. Many A-list influencers (and even traditional journalists) won't notice an idea until lesser, yet influential peers write about it. This "Magic Middle" tier of influencers, as Technorati founder David Sifry dubbed them in 2006,[102] often breaks stories that trickle up until a "Connector" or A-List blogger discovers them.

On the other hand, major influencers can fan an ember into a raging inferno. Consider how famous blogger Robert Scoble tweeted the China earthquake in 2008 to the world. Scoble actually received word from several people within China on Twitter. After seeing the story come from several sources, he relayed the news to his massive social network. As a result, Scoble beat even the U.S. Geological Survey with news about the disaster—a great example of the Fifth Estate at work.[103]

Many times you have to tickle an idea up the grapevine to the major A-listers, who often are late to embrace a story. However, once they do write something, there is great potential for word of mouth to spread through their trusting communities, either with traditional media or further social media conversations.

No one knows what's going to go "viral." But talking to the few and the passionate—your influencers, often leaders in the community—is always an ingredient, often at an early stage, but certainly at some point during the upward trending curve. For organizational social media, this means building credible relationships with contacts who have networks of the right people, not necessarily the most people. Understanding your community's dynamics and building relationships from within as a member of the Fifth Estate is a much more reliable strategy than buying a list. In the next chapter, you'll find tips on tactical interaction with online influencers.

Empowering the Community Through Crowdsourcing

The mark of a great social media effort is when the community itself owns it. We can use lighter fluid and kindling, we can light the match, we can fan the flames, but only the Fifth Estate can make our issue, our movement, burn with the full fire of an inferno. When the community embraces and takes on a topic as its own beyond an organization's efforts, word of mouth occurs in its most complex and desirable form.

Our job as organizational communicators lies in trying to facilitate a larger conversation by empowering people to share content and initiate discussions. A movement compels people to make a cause or product a part of their lives, not just their Facebook profiles. It's always better to have 500 people screaming about one's wares than 5,000 passive followers who may see a Tweet. Instead of thinking about how to get 1,000 people into your Facebook group, think about how you can use your Facebook group to engage your peers, change your work environment and spark a movement of people who are incredibly passionate about your issues.

One of the hotter memes in online empowerment today is the crowdsourcing trend.[104] Sparked by recent cause marketing (consider the Pepsi Refresh contest) and product development successes (for example, Cisco's I-Prize initiative), everyone wants to talk about crowdsourcing as the new ultimate result of the social web. But the crowd is not always trustworthy, creating a need for strong community-management skills so an organization can elicit productive results.[105]

Smart crowdsourcing efforts should have a well-defined purpose. Whether that's ending hunger or developing new products, smart crowdsourcing seeks to achieve a goal, not just create a splash. Without a common purpose, the crowd is rudderless. Even with a purpose, projects need a significant amount of community management to keep on track.

Cisco's I-Prize attracted more than 2,500 innovators— entrants from 104 countries submitted 1,200 distinct ideas for next-generation Internet technologies. Said Cisco's Guido Jouret: "The evaluation process was far more labor-intensive than we'd anticipated; significant investments of time, energy, patience and imagination are required to discern the gems hidden within rough stones. Anyone attempting to do innovation on the cheap should look elsewhere."[106]

One of the limitations with Pepsi Refresh, although it's a brilliant crowdsourcing campaign, is its lack of stated purpose. There's no theory of change. Instead, the mission is strictly cause marketing, trusted to the crowd's popular choices for good ideas: "Pepsi is giving away millions to fund great ideas." The end result is a free-for-all of people and organizations trying to get the prizes—a carnival-like popularity contest. The measurable social outcomes have yet to be revealed by Pepsi, and indeed, it's likely the only measurements will be strictly in brand equity and sales as the cola company has focused on how many votes and impressions it is getting, and not how it is impacting society.

With a stated purpose, community managers can guide their crowds toward a common mission. Crowdsource participants understand the product's motives, yet feel comfortable participating—whether out of brand loyalty, the desire for recognition, interest in the project or to win a final prize.

Community management is not crowd control, which is well-nigh impossible in social communities. A crowdsourcing effort provides a welcoming environment that enables people to participate freely. It makes them feel good to take part in the project and adds something to their lives. Community managers should suggest ways to achieve a successful outcome, but members should be free to do as they wish, within acceptable behavioral boundaries (for example, please do not use inappropriate language). In that sense, community members have the opportunity to do as well, or as poorly, as they choose.[107] The manager is much more of a horse whisperer, coaxing Fifth Estate members toward a useful end.

This means crowdsourcing as a strategic choice requires time and resources in addition to an organization's other social media approaches. Sometimes that investment can be minimal —using the community as an informal focus group, asking for ideas. But in instances such as Cisco's "I-Prize," crowdsourcing can take a formidable amount of work.

Many large companies and nonprofit groups have the same issues with crowdsourcing within their own walls. Their efforts are so scattered that any centralized social media effort is almost impossible. Instead, their management model may empower local stores, chapters and managers to act as if they are their own Fifth Estate members within certain guidelines. Rather than trying to control social media efforts under one roof, they use networked models to empower individual stakeholders in the larger organization using a hive-like framework. A networked model for an organization assumes and includes the following:

• Lack of control on the local frontline.

• An engaged internal community manager who will use social tools and help networked affiliates as requested.

• A corporate-built framework of tools include social network and blogging platforms, graphics, tagging guidelines and social media best-practice training and guidelines.

• A corresponding, overarching corporate initiative that embodies best practices.

• Combating "wayward" efforts with suggestions for betterment rather than enforcement.

• Continuing commitments by headquarters to highlight local case studies and enhance, better and promote the framework.

In addition to building the actual framework, a great deal of the effort involves internal alliance-building and communications. Local stakeholders need to be made aware of and convinced of the effectiveness of the social media tool sets.

Consider the 2008 Obama presidential campaign's

social media efforts. Partisan politics aside, Obama's campaign communications involved intense grassroots activities using social media tools. Tens of thousands of Obama campaigners, advocates and even casual voters were enabled to spread the message. At the heart of the effort was activism on more than a dozen social networks, as well as the Obama campaign's website. Bloggers using the Obama platform even posted negatively against proposals or Obama actions.[108]

It was not your average political campaign, but it did fit into the networked model. The result speaks for itself.

CHAPTER FOUR SNAPSHOTS

Creating a communications strategy involves determinating of your goals building the plan to achieve those goals, and selecting the tools you likely will use. Strategy within social media is required because of its two-way nature, requiring a unique set of tools. However, it is unwise to isolate it from the rest of your communications strategy, because the Fourth and Fifth Estates are intrinsically linked.

Positioning your offering or social action in a clear, streamlined fashion is a crucial aspect of forging your strategy. Listening and research are keys to developing an informed strategy to ensure your success.

Shiny Object Syndrome

It's important to vet your strategy for Shiny Object Syndrome. If you find yourself talking about the tools; i.e. Facebook pages and iPad apps, without first having your outcomes, positioning strategy and general approach outlined, then you probably are experimenting instead of communicating.

Participation Is Marketing

"Participation is marketing" means that getting involved in the community and doing more than talking helps your organization build relationships. Showing a human face, demonstrating a larger conversation than messaging and showing interest in others can produce a wide range of intangible benefits.

The Editorial Mission: A Commitment to Service

Social media content works best when it is designed to serve specific stakeholders. Employing an editorial mission keeps an organization on track with its service commitment to the community. Applications and websites that succeed keep a singular focus and avoid spammy, sales-like approaches.

Influencer Relations

Many organizations build relationships with crucial influencers and hope the communities following those leading voices will follow suit. However, making this happen takes more than buying a list, because many top influencers are fed content and ideas by their social networks.

Empowerment

Empowerment assumes that the organization will commit to building a far-flung community. Empowerment strategies create conversations and ideas that are so extensive that they exist well beyond the organization's reach. Crowdsourcing is the most common example of the empowerment strategy, but managing it requires substantial time and guidance. Large organizational efforts need empowerment guidelines across far-flung operations.

Chapter 5
Promotion Within Your Community

Now that you've forged your strategy, it's time to mingle with the Fifth Estate! Go out there, forge relationships, and see how the long tail of media can impact your organization.

First, understand that a "build it and they will come" attitude could keep your effort from reaching its fullest potential. Additionally, launching it with an "us vs. them" mentality will immediately segregate the community— beginning its demise before it can flourish. These two no-nos are hallmarks of the old, command-and-control approach to messaging and communications.

This crystallized for me when Ike Pigott first said that social media was an organic process.[109] His statement struck me as inherently true, in large part because of the significant amount of time and care one has to invest in building an active community. Like farmers who invest love and labor day after day watching their fields slowly yield beautiful fruits and vegetables, community developers must tend to their communities and build relationships through thoughtful interactions, valuable content and empowerment methods.

Most marketers and communicators fail to realize the imperative of engaging the Fifth Estate as a group of people just like them. Instead they analyze their consumers as a group to exploit and focus on how major online media like Google and Facebook have changed with widespread adoption.[110] They obsess with the business objective and cannot grasp the human context.

I have a friend, Meryl Steinberg, who says that when she signed on to Twitter and Facebook, she didn't sign on to be a consumer. Her sentiments mirror many others' on social networks; they find themselves assaulted with marketers' messages trying to persuade them of the values of their products or causes.

These communicators analyze the data, looking for the big score. They hope, even expect, that when they launch their social media, the results will become their own version of the Haiti text-based fundraising phenomenon and raise tens of millions of dollars,[111] or that they can reproduce the viral success of Old Spice's "Old Spice Man" videos.[112] These social ads featured a bare-chested, sculpted man telling ladies what they want in a man, and then responding to social community inquiries via YouTube and Twitter posts. Communicator might never replicate this success. In reality, their best chance is to build a loyal community that eagerly looks forward to initiatives from the organization, and then launch an effort that infuses that special mix of creativity, intentional stakeholder-centric approach, and, yes—timing.

When the engine starts and engagement begins, often the Fifth Estate does not respond. The seeds have only begun to be planted. Loyal relationships don't sprout overnight. A vast majority of organizations don't experience immediate success online.

The road can be long and hard, and at times, communicators can feel like they are walking through a desert, hoping desperately to find an oasis of engagement. This is the point at which many organizations quit and let their social effort lie fallow.

It's important not to minimize the effort and time that must be invested to build and then to sustain a community. The Fifth Estate requires continued interactions; the time and human-resource commitments are significant. Have the patience to see it through from start to finish, to forge ahead through the dry spells that lie between moments of fruitful interaction.

The social media environment is filling with more and more businesses and nonprofits seeking to engage their various communities, creating competition for the Fifth Estate's attention. Members are used to getting hit up for sales, donations, click-throughs and the dissemination of messages. They usually turn deaf ears to such blatant efforts.

To help attract members of the Fifth Estate to the important conversation you'd like to hold with them, you'll need a community relations program. Relationships will need to be developed with influencers and regular folks, as well.

While some of these tactics are conventional, they

should all be used in the spirit of participation within the community—based on service, relationships and trust. In essence, the attitude must be one of approaching peers, listening and then providing value, rather than generating leads or selling product. The measurable and desirable outcome any organization seeks —return on investment— should be considered a by-product of successfully interacting with your community, a result of providing valuable insights and information to them. In essence, help them and they'll help you.

The following tactical areas represent some of the more common methods of interaction across different forms of social technology. These general areas range from the simplest to the most complex.

This book means to provide you the information necessary for leadership, for empowering champions for change and for building your organization's community with some general approaches. To help you lead through an effort, here are some main aspects of tactical outreach that work.

If strategy is a plan to achieve a desired goal (A to B), then tactics represent the actions of engagement. In a social media sense, tactical mastery is the art of contacting and interacting with your stakeholders using the outreach and tools you have chosen.

Note that Facebook is not a tactic. The use of Facebook is. More specifically, tactics cause you to examine whether you are publishing messages or asking questions of your community. Is activity strictly limited to your page, or are you writing on the walls of your important community members? Are you sharing useful information or merely asking people to attend your event? The actions you employ on Facebook represent your tactical execution.

As you frame social media tactics in this light, there are many general actions to consider:

Conversation Starters: Do you use conversation-starters or messages?

Relationship Approaches: How are your interactions with others? In a relationship-oriented media, it's about other-centric behavior.

Shareability: If you built something, from a simple widget or blog to an application or social network, how social is the design? Is it easy to use, open and share?

Integration: How well does your social effort integrate into your larger communications plan?

Influencer Relationship Development: Are you building relationships to last or spamming your influencers?

Community Management: Are you using principles to encourage the community to absorb your subject matter and make it theirs? Or are you dominating the conversation?

Course Correction: Sometimes even the best planning can't anticipate how the community will react. That's when you adapt. Is your effort flexible enough to change course?

Reputation Management: What will you do when the Fifth Estate disagrees and openly questions your position?

These questions apply to just about every social media outreach effort. And that's not including the specific use of tools and their best practices. You'll need to know the ins and outs of your preferred social media networks, publishing engines, applications and widgets, too.

Conversation Starters: A Modern View of Messaging

Organizational messaging has been under fire for a long time from many a PR 2.0/social media/web 2.0 pundit, including me. While the Cluetrain principle that there's no market for messages discussed in Chapter 1 is a critical theory that drives much of the two-way conversation online, more evolved messaging has its place: starting the conversation.

When engaging the Fifth Estate, a good message doesn't drill home a sales proposition, highlight a brand attribute or control public perception. Instead it inspires a great conversation among community members. It's a conversational lead, something that provokes raw dialogue about an issue that is relevant, not only to the organization providing the starter, but also to the community participating in the discussion.[113]

In that sense the modern message isn't controlled. It's actually crafted with the hope of sparking a wildfire of uncontrolled word of mouth. That means giving people something worthwhile to talk about.

So a message actually becomes Socratic in nature. It poses a question and/or causes other parties to actually think about a topic, as opposed to trying to force proscribed ideas into their heads. Social web messages can start the conversation, but they may not end them.[114]

In fact the community conversation may turn the message upside down. Many brands have experienced this, including Apple and AT&T with iPhone pricing, Domino's Pizza and Motrin Moms. In such cases, an organization needs to respond to and be flexible with its community. That's where loosening the reins and actively participating in dialogue really comes into play. If the message serves the community with informative conversation, then the organization that started the community should understand that it may need to shift its position.

Approaches Toward Building Relationships

When asked to recommend a book for social media, sometimes I'll quip, "How to Win Friends and Influence People." It only seems amusing. Kidding aside, Dale Carnegie's principles have stood the test of time because they provide sound guidelines for fostering better relationships.[115]

For the United Way's Staff Leaders Conference in 2009, social media leader Meg Keaney and I presented best practices for tactical social networking. We decided to embed and apply Dale Carnegie's principles to three of the main social networks: Facebook, LinkedIn and Twitter.[116] We walked our participants through applying these suggestions online.

We just scratched the surface on how to apply Dale Carnegie's principles to social media. The ways to create great relationships online are endless. Yet it's this kind of tactical engagement that makes or breaks online campaigns. The importance of successfully strengthening relationships with influencers, customers, donors, volunteers and other members of the Fifth Estate cannot be overestimated. It's the equivalent of editing, spell-checking, and re-editing an important document before releasing it to the public.

Case Study: Samuel Gordon Jewelers

Oklahoma City-based Samuel Gordon Jewelers is a family-owned, 106-year-old company. Fourth-generation owner Dan Gordon took over the company in the mid 1990s; he always has had a fascination with the World

Wide Web. In 2004, the company was spending as much as $500,000 on its traditional advertising budget, and that's when Gordon began experimenting with social web tools, primarily using a participation strategy.[117]

"The motto I've lived by in real life and online is the same: 'Give everything you've got, and you will get more back than you ever thought,' " Gordon said. "What that means to me is several things. I learn from others, hopefully I give value of what I learn and know myself, and, in turn, the cycle continuously repeats itself. To make a long story short, I stay unselfish, un-self-centered, and try to make sure that people know who the real me is, and I give more back than I receive."[118]

Engagement

Dan's social efforts began with a Wedding to Remember in 2004, a crowdsourced contest that saw locals voting on his website. The nine-month post tripled his website traffic, encouraging Gordon to do more.

Next came a blog that engaged customers in a very successful dialogue. Then Twitter and Facebook rolled around, and Gordon built a following that comes for the conversation and then become interested in specials. Gordon is the voice of the company on the social web, giving top-level access and continuing the tradition of a family-owned business.

When mobile came around, Gordon added an iPhone and Android application that allow people to sound off on different jewelry conversations. Samuel Gordon Jewelers has even added a "mayor special" for people checking in on mobile geolocation-based social network Foursquare.

Results

Since 2004 Dan Gordon's foot traffic has increased by 30%, while he has used social media tools as the primary thrust of his outreach effort. He still uses traditional media to promote his business, but his advertising budget has been cut by 90% to $50,000.[119]

"What I liked about Dan's focus on, and incorporation of, social media is that he remains grounded in how it will impact his business," said Shonali Burke, a marketing consultant who wrote a case study about Samuel Gordon Jewelers. "That does not, however, detract from his understanding of the conversational and connection element of the medium. Rather, it reinforces his use of it, which is precisely why he has been able to reduce his ad spend as dramatically as he explained when I profiled him on BNET.[120]"

Gordon continues to innovate. At the time of writing, he was working on crowdsourcing initiatives, including customer-created ads, and figuring out how to layer mobile geolocation activities to make the game aspects more enjoyable. "The future plans are to see what works, analyze results as they accumulate, find new ways to grow community and convert more," Gordon said.[121]

Design

Shareability is using online site design and applications that "plug in" to your website to ensure that Fifth Estate members can easily share your content, information and anything else they want to share on your site. Whether they want to share the information on their social network, on their blog or with their e-mail contacts, you want people to be able to do this with as few mouse clicks as possible—ideally no more than two.

From a technology perspective, an organization can do much to embrace "shareability." Specifically, there are great software plug-ins such as AddThis!, ShareThis, and FaceBook's OpenGraph (Like) that let anyone port content just about anywhere. OpenGraph's shareability has empowered Facebook to separate itself from the pack, and it is rapidly becoming the dominant social network of the new decade. Facebook has surpassed Google in web traffic.

From a policy and approach standpoint, shareability means highlighting customer and volunteer stories. It may even mean acknowledging a customer complaint or issue on the main site. But the general ethos should be empowering stakeholders and making them feel good for becoming a part of your core community. That builds loyalty and movements, and it makes people feel good about associating with your brand.

A classic concern for traditional organizations is copyright and intellectual property rights. In most instances, shareability and grassroots communications should supersede concerns about plagiarism of your content. It's a question of which will have more impact, defending your rights or spreading your contributions to community dialogue. In cases where intellectual property should be protected, technologies like Adobe PDF and sites like Flickr, Scribd and Slideshare can protect your social content with intellectual property licensing while empowering people to access it electronically.

Integration: Leverage Your Current Marketing Activities

There's a cliché in the advertising business that you have to touch customers seven times (this number varies depending on the source) through a variety of mechanisms to get them to act. Regardless of the actual number, it's important to use different media forms to promote your social media effort.

People don't go home and say to themselves, "Hmm, I think I'll go consume some social media, then write something so I can become a member of the Fifth Estate." They don't think about it. People drift from print to TV to electronic media and back without parsing their media choices. Their picture of information and the brands that are introduced to them through the media is seamless. They may not even remember, and likely don't care, where they first heard of a product or company.

So smart organizations serve their stakeholders through several media channels. They know it's necessary to garner mindshare.

For example, in 2007, for the first time, several Super Bowl ads like Doritos invited viewers to related websites for user-generated content and contests. In some cases the ads were selected or created by participants within the company's social media community. [122]

In 2010, Pepsi diverted its Super Bowl advertising budget to crowdsourced community projects promoted via social media power users and causes that rallied their networks to become the most popular. Pepsi's Refresh project involves more than online communications, including public-relations pitches to traditional media, radio and TV ad buys, event sponsorships and more; it's a well-publicized and advertised outreach campaign.

These advertisers know that social media users access information through a variety of mechanisms, so they communicated using an integrated outreach effort. Some simple, obvious ways to promote a blog or other new media initiative include:

- Signatures at the end of an email
- Prominent links on main websites

- Email or letters of introduction to existing contact databases
- Direct mail
- Advertising
- References during media interviews
- Links in newsletters promising related, value-added content
- URL on business cards and stationery
- Inclusion within corporate brochures and collateral

All of these channels can alert online users to your conversations. If you attract their curiosity, you've opened an opportunity to engage in dialogue and build a more loyal community. In some cases you might even migrate current consumers of traditional media communications to new media. Even more, online communities is no longer the stuff of Millenials and Generation X with 42% of adults older than 50 using social media tools in May 2010.[123]

While not all traditional media consumers will migrate to your new content and the value you've created for them, some will. Migration toward social media is inevitable as the form becomes more dominant. And by helping or making your community aware of your organization's effort, you build value in your outreach efforts with an even larger community.

Outreach: Pitching to New Media Outlets

There's much debate about communicating directly with influencers. The classic marketing mistake still is addressing influencers with traditional media methods. New media voices do not have any obligation to "report" or field inquiries, they don't have to write a kind review of your product (even if you comp them something), and a great majority distrust traditional public relations tactics.

Influencers determine how they want to be contacted. Keep in mind their role as an independent voice in the information world. Try focusing on building relationships over time. Create value for them in relation to their work or their lives, talk to them about the things that they care about and help them achieve their goals. By doing these things and generally building a stronger social network with influencers embedded as hubs in your ongoing interaction, you become more effective.

Unless strong social network relationships are in play, news that may be of interest to a community cannot be communicated naturally and virally. This weakens an organization's or company's position because it forces marketing to push initiatives onto influencers rather than attract their attention. Social media is not receptive to this kind of promotion.

A strong social network strategy, or providing value to a network, links Fifth Estate members to the organization's efforts. If they believe in the organization, they often are willing to help promote it. A dialogue already exists, so it's okay to tell your social network about an exciting new development—as long as it's of interest to them.

The Gap's gift of clothes to the female blogging community before the BlogHer conference is a good example of engaging a community in this manner. The Gap understood that it had something of value (new professional clothing) to offer the bloggers.

"Regardless of the industry segment or specific details of the campaign, the best influencer relations programs have one thing in common: the value exchange between brand

and influencer is balanced," said author Susan Getgood. "Each gives something of value to the other, both are satisfied with the exchange and nobody feels taken advantage of."[124]

Experience demonstrates that a very simple pitch drawn up for new media outlets should be customized to each individual. It's better to reach out to 50 individuals than to group blast 500 with a news release. As with media relations, customized intelligent pitching, particularly when there may be a preexisting relationship, has a higher rate of success.

Any pitch should be clear about the new media outlet's interest and must provide value to the influencer by offering information that corresponds to that interest. One example is early trials of products or services. Be prepared, however, for less-than-rave reviews. If the information is poor, you certainly can expect a negative write-up. On the other hand, you could gain insights that elude traditional market research. It's also often suggested that no pitch overtly demand or request a post, but instead should provide an "FYI" only or a request for help.

The pitch is usually sent as a private message, emailed or presented as a tip submitted through a web form on the social media site—if the site invites tips. Once you send your pitch, let it go. Do not follow up or harass community members or bloggers. Pressure equals bad write-ups about your organization.

If you've talked to enough people and there's no pick-up or interest, take it as a sign that your organization isn't creating enough value for your community or that your relationships are not in order, and be happy you didn't get slammed by one of the bloggers. Begin again by building value for the community instead of trying to exploit its members by pitching them.

Fostering Strong Community

What about communities within and beyond the oft-talked-about majors like Twitter, Facebook, YouTube and Flickr? "How does one engage," is a very common question. There are general principles that apply across all social communities, major or not.

Some of these tenets are obvious, human behaviors that, when exhibited in a two-way conversation, can turn users off. Some are best practices learned from mistakes and based on actions others have taken.

1) Return to your site. Be smart, especially if you are building a community within a larger network. If you want to build relationships with people, give them a way to contact you and perhaps further engage. Provide intelligent calls to action. Post meaningful links and content that your community members may want to see. Then provide avenues for those who want to develop an even stronger relationship with you.

Many companies and nonprofits do well in branding and awareness on major social networks, but they fail to achieve significant relationship development. They only publish content on Facebook and Twitter. Getting people to interact with you on your site is the difference-maker here. The numbers are smaller, but the relationships are stronger.

2) Let them lead. A common mistake is to over-communicate and attempt to dominate your social media. Rather, foster an environment in which at some point the conversation takes off and community members become activated, seeking to lead conversations themselves. It's at this point that the organization has achieved grassroots activism or brand evangelism. So let them lead.

This transfer of roles is delicate. Your organization is seeking to shift from conversation starter to community facilitator. An apropos metaphor is hosting a party. Be a non-meddling host who lets guests enjoy the company and ambience. No one likes a host who seeks to dominate every interaction.

3) Play within existing communities. It doesn't make sense most of the time to create your own community. In fact, most organizationally originated communities fail.[125] Usually an appropriate community already exists on Ning, a community bulletin board or, yes, one of the majors. Explore where open application programming interfaces (APIs), value-added content and groups will let you play within a larger community rather than immediately seeking to create your own network.

Consider how HubSpot created Twitter Grader, a service that ranked Twitter users' individual clout, then used that data to produce the "State of the Twittersphere" report.[126] Hubspot also produces inbound marketing software, a natural tie to their value proposition for stakeholders who need to report data—and need to know how to build a successful application like Twitter Grader.

4) Work with the community. Another somewhat obvious personal relations skill is recognizing that an organization's users are also its partners.[127] Companies like Southwest Airlines have figured out how to use their social communities to vet significant changes.[128] Partnering with community members keeps them engaged and further increases their loyalty. This increases exponentially when you publicly acknowledge and reward their successes.

5) Stay relevant. Sometimes communities grow stale. Keep updating the technical prowess, features, content and capabili-

ties that are feeding your community. Consider the updates that networks like Twitter and Facebook make every year, and sometimes more frequently, to keep their network relevant. When platforms change, your effort is inadvertently affected because you need to adapt with the community. Sometimes changes like this cause the community to leave, as the Digg crowdsourcing news network found out when it over-managed user behavior that created top news stories.

Most of these tactical best practices make common sense when you consider them in the context of personal relationships. You can never go wrong with "Golden Rule"-based actions and principles.

Case Study: Plum Village

The Unified Buddhist Church, commonly known as the Plum Village International Sangha and personified in Zen Master Thich Nhat Hanh, launched a social media presence approximately one year before a 2009 U.S. Teaching Tour. Led by Nobel Peace Prize nominee Thich Nhat Hanh, the effort was launched using Twitter and Facebook in an effort to reach a broader, and younger, audience of people who are interested in mindfulness practice but who may not frequent static web pages.

"The goal was not lofty, but simply to put the voice of Thich Nhat Hanh into the new social media environment," said the online architect of the effort, Kenley Neufeld, who is a lay practitioner ordained in the Unified Buddhist Church. "I wanted to reach a new, younger, non-Buddhist audience. People who can practice mindfulness. Anyone."

Engagement

Launched on Facebook and Twitter in 2008, the social media efforts were integrated into e-mail distribution lists and on traditional web pages. The online audience for the Thich Nhat Hanh branded accounts grew in ways that were unexpected, and it grew fast. The initial demographics represented groups not typical of those who came to retreats. They revealed many more young people and a better balance of male and female followers.

"What's really happened is that a conversation is taking place between audience members," said Neufeld. "They talk to each other. Discuss. Explore concepts and ideas together. The 'official' page can really take a back seat and allow for the conversation to take place on its own."

The traditional community wasn't too keen on the Twitter/Facebook stuff. However, monastics appreciate Facebook because it connects them to their brothers and sisters in the different centers across the globe, so in many ways they are leading the way. This is evident in the development of online monasteries. Both the voices of newcomers to Buddhism and longer-term practitioners are included in the conversation.

Outcomes

The biggest outcome for the Unified Buddhist Church and Neufeld was the ability to reach audiences. On the 2009 tour, the Colorado event was the largest retreat on the U.S. tour ever—with 900 attendees—and the dynamic experience spawned a new book, *One Buddha Is Not Enough.* Today, the volunteer effort has a significant Facebook community with more than 160,000 members.

As a result of these successes, there is a new movement to create an online monastery where people can hear and practice the dharma at a distance. Additional forms of online media are being incorporated into the church's efforts. Thich Nhat Hanh has encouraged this and provided the resources (monastics and money) to help make it happen.

The group is purchasing computers, cloud servers and other resources.

Two of the other centers in the Order of Interbeing tradition (Deer Park Monastery and European Institute of Applied Buddhism) have created Facebook pages where they are interacting with the audience. Deer Park, in particular, has started an "Ask a Dharma Teacher" effort though Facebook. For the most recent Southeast Asian Teaching Tour, the church is livestreaming its efforts. In addition, it continues its Facebook and Twitter initiatives to share live dharma talks by including quotes and key concepts through the social media environment.

Course Correction

Sometimes you find yourself in the middle of the outreach effort, and results are lagging. Measurable outcomes based on your original objectives seem unattainable. Your organic community development seems to be lost in the Sahara, and fear creeps in.

That's when to consider a course correction. Does a course correction represent a failure?

Maybe. Maybe not. For organizations that are relative newcomers to online communities, the need to shift can result from not fully understanding how the Fifth Estate disagrees on a questionable matter, or perhaps stems from a need to fine-tune an application so it's easier to use.

Sometimes a strategic choice is simply off-base; the organization overestimated the value it offered. The issues that arose over KFC's 2010 offering of pink fried chicken buckets to benefit cancer research fundraiser Komen represents a classic example of this disconnect. Obesity is a risk factor for breast cancer among older women, according to research linked to on the Komen website. So many in the nonprofit blogging community saw the Komen/KFC partnership as inappropriate or hypocritical. When challenged about it, KFC chose to continue without changing course and reaped negative posts that became indexed in Google.

What is clear is that monitoring measurements (discussed in depth in the next chapter) during outreach should tune you in and help you to head off possible failures and recognize opportunities for optimization. When these issues are identified, not making a course correction can be the worst failure of all.

Reputation Management

Difficulties arise. Mistakes happen. Reputations become tarnished—this is the way of the world, particularly when an error occurs after a company brand achieves a leadership position or a human being becomes famous. As we've seen time and time again, when a problem is avoided or "hushed up," the blemish becomes more pronounced. But when the setback is embraced, reputation damage can be ameliorated and in some cases, even reversed.

While an enraged Fifth Estate creates accelerated brand damage for organizations, conversational media can mollify angry customers or perturbed fans with direct interaction. Further, demonstrating responsiveness can help reputation management via online searching. When people see response to criticism and a commitment to resolve issues after public outcries, they are much more likely to believe the company cares about its customers.

Perhaps the most storied example of this is Dell's magnificent use of its blog when laptop batteries were literally blowing up, setting their laptops on fire.[130] By embracing the issue, Dell went a long way toward resolving the matter and defusing anger directed at the brand. Robert Downey Jr. and MC Hammer (an online media star in his own right) are great examples of individuals who recovered their reputations after being tarnished.

On the other hand, failure to engage creates its own issues. Pop icon Prince found out that the worst way to handle these situations is attempting to force fans (and commenters) to retract statements. Message control in social media environments doesn't work; two-way conversational capabilities have permanently closed the door on that strategy.

When Prince tried to shut down three united, fan-generated sites to protect copyrighted material, fans dug in their heels. One fan wrote to prince.org: "The more I think about it, I say just drop him, remove all content, let him have his way. It's obvious he doesn't want us as fans anymore, so why should we want him?" Instead of quelling the storm, actions like Prince's attempts to control the use of his image and media tend to incite increased hostility.[131]

When a crisis occurs, successful communication efforts employ factual, timely updates. Organizations admit their fault and take public steps to address the issue. Such times can offer a company the opportunity to shine and actually build goodwill with its community.

Applying these principles to negative comments can achieve similar results. When the popcorn industry faced a diacetyl crisis—reports that a flavoring used in popcorn products was linked to lung disease in its workers—parent bloggers were incensed, concerned that they had been feeding their children a cancer causing food. Smart organic popcorn companies engaged bloggers directly by posting comments. These companies didn't even have a social media presence but together unified to respond to concerned voices. They acknowledged the issue for mainstream popcorn brands, but also highlighted brands that did not use diacetyl as an ingredient. Within a day the incident was quelled.

Some of the lessons learned from all of these incidents include:

• Respond promptly. Days are too long when minutes and hours can create an uprising on the Internet.

• Acknowledge wrongs or problems and the steps taken to correct them.

• Publish a co-joining statement on their blog or website.

• Don't apologize and then repeat your errors.

• If someone is complaining, and the company can't effect change, acknowledge their remarks. Make them feel heard.

Remember that smaller members of the Fifth Estate matter, too. A common mistake is to ignore remarks on blogs and social networks with less traffic, assuming they're too small and don't matter. What if a more influential blogger or a journalist reads a small site and picks up the story? Influence is also determined by who reads the post, not just by quantity of readers.

At the same time, an inevitable byproduct of success is the attraction of negative elements. Aptly dubbed "trolls," these folks attack no matter what you do. If the negative commenter is a troll, usually a Google search will reveal a litany of negativity.

The best thing to do with trolls is to ignore them. Do not comment on their sites; engaging trolls only fuels them. If they attack in the comments sections of other sites, then respond—but only as it pertains to the general post, not the troll's remarks. Remember, they seek attention. While the comment may seem worthy of deletion by your policy, deletion can just further fuel attacks.[134]

Interested readers who click through to a troll's site will see the general negativity and should be able to exercise good judgment. They may even Google the person in question and find the same results you did.

Of course, if threats are made, follow up with law enforcement. Then uber-popular blogger Kathy Sierra received death threats in 2008 from a few wayward followers. She notified the authorities who discovered the perpetrators. Similarly, if continued blatant defamation and libel occur, the company or individual may want to consider legal action. Usually, if you don't take the bait, the troll will move on to another target.

CHAPTER FIVE SNAPSHOTS

Social media communication requires a significant investment of time; it is an organic process that can take months, even years to reach fruition. Organizations need to invest patience in cultivating their online stakeholders. Getting there requires a focus on tactical performance and maximizing interactions with the Fifth Estate.

Conversation Starters

Instead of trying to deliver messages, use your strategic positioning to create a conversation starter. Well-crafted, intentional and inviting of dialogue, these initial forays should inspire the Fifth Estate to engage with your organization.

Approaches To Relationship Building

Fostering relationships requires an other-centric approach that engages people in ways that foster likeability and positive emotional bonds. This is the basic "blocking and tackling" of social media. Enduring principles such as those presented in Dale Carnegie's *How to Win Friends and Influence People* can help an organization focus on strengthening ties to others through modern social networks such as LinkedIn, Facebook and Twitter.

Design for Shareability

Good tactical website design encourages sharing of your content in every way possible. Use widgets and applications to empower members of the Fifth Estate to port your data and information any way they would like, with a minimal number of clicks. From an intellectual property standpoint, weigh the benefits of grassroots communication versus that of protecting ideas. Usually sharing content and ideas is more valuable.

Integrate Your Communications

People do not delineate their media consumption, so why should you? The Fifth Estate still holds business cards, watches TV programs, reads e-mail and hears radio ads.

Integrating social media into your larger communications program dramatically increases the likelihood that your organization will make an impression on important stakeholders.

Influencer Relations

Building relationships with influencers remains a crucial aspect of online communications, regardless of the social media form. Keep in mind that influencers have no obligation to write about your organization. Focus on building value for them and demonstrating how your effort best affects them and their communities.

Fostering Community Ties

Managing the community requires paying close attention to and fostering stronger ties with your loyal members. Strengthen ties by bringing them back to your site, listening to their feedback, empowering them to make decisions and run groups. Seek them out where they already congregate on the main social networks, and work to stay relevant to their evolving conversation.

Course Correction

Using measurement benchmarks, you can tell if your online campaign is off the mark or can use some tweaking. Almost every online effort requires adaptation; success is contingent upon paying attention to the signs and adjusting as necessary.

Reputation Management

Sometimes the Fifth Estate takes issue with your organization. Rather than shutting down or enforcing controlled communications, crisis PR tenets are very helpful in online communications. It's important to respond, and to do so factually. When you're in the wrong, prompt amends should be made. It's important to vet and handle negative factors as well.

Chapter 6
A Common-Sense Approach to Measuring Social Media

A chapter guest-written by Kami Watson Huyse, APR

The problem with communication and relationships, which both are hallmarks of social media, is the difficulty of quantifying their effects. Most people don't connect online efforts to bottom-line sales, funds raised or other business results, or even to softer measures such as improved relationships and competitive advantage. Because of this, organizations tend to measure the easy stuff in social media—follower counts, blog traffic, rankings and, if they are really sophisticated, engagement measures such as the number of comments on Facebook or a blog, retweets and mentions on Twitter, links to their blog or website and other such indicators of attention.

There are three camps of thought about measuring the effectiveness of social media: the "Measurement Naysayers" on the left, the "Bean Counters" on the right and the "Measurement Explorers" somewhere in the middle.

The Naysayers eschew measurement, calling it antithetical to the ethos of social media. This camp says that each individual voice is important and that all input should be seen as valuable. It feels that by measuring, an organization sets up a transactional relationship instead of building a more desirable, egalitarian one. On the opposite side of the divide are the Bean Counters, those who say that business results should drive the involvement of an organization in social media. They are not very interested in the softer measures of influence, reputation or relationship building. Their focus is return on investment (ROI), and they don't see the point of wasting valuable resources on something that doesn't contribute to the bottom line.

The third camp, which we will call the social media measurement "Explorers," falls somewhere in between the other two and is happy to look at multiple measures to show the efficacy of social media. While a monetary return is the primary objective, there are a variety of ways to measure the impact that social media channels have on advancing the goals of the business or nonprofit. This moderate view is the most common-sense approach for social spaces and usually yields the best results.

In reality, people fall all along this continuum of measurement philosophies, and each organization needs to look for the right balance. However, the more an organization moves toward the middle ground and becomes an explorer, the more likely it will achieve success. It's hard to run a business or nonprofit on good feelings alone, and conversely, facilitating word-of-mouth advocacy will be difficult if the goal is to convert every touch into a transaction.

Measurement as a Diagnostic Tool

As was laid out so well in the first thesis of the *Cluetrain Manifesto*[135], the classic book at the forefront of the social media movement, "Markets are conversations." People increasingly demand that companies and nonprofits wake up from their slumber and connect with them. Or as the authors say: "You want us to pay? We want you to pay attention."

Of course, organizations must make money to survive, and that is where a social media measurement program can help determine where to focus money, time and effort in a way that also recognizes that markets want organizations to engage. At its most basic level, a measurement program is a diagnostic tool. Rather than seeking to squeeze the last drop of profit from every customer engaged in a social networking context, measurements should be used to determine if a social media strategy is working, if it needs adjustment and where it should be adjusted. They also should take into account the softer assets that social media can bring to the table, such as improved client or stakeholder relationships, organizational reputation and competitive advantage.

Moreover, measurement of social media, as with all communication efforts, helps to quantify its value to the organization. In a blog post about the report "Social Marketing Analytics, A New Framework for Measuring Results in Social Media,"[136] Jeremiah Owyang, industry analyst for the Altimeter Group, explains the importance of a measurement strategy:

> While experiments can fly under the radar for a short term, without having a measurement strategy you run the risk of not improving what you're doing, justifying investments

and the appearance of being aloof to upper management. To be successful, all programs (even new media) must have a measurement strategy.[137]

A well-thought-out measurement strategy can justify the loftier goal of engagement and relationship-building activities that social media are so good at brokering. If an organization can demonstrate loyalty, increased sales, decreased marketing costs, reduced customer service calls, improved reputation and a number of other measures, it can make a persuasive argument that digital marketing and social networking are worthwhile.

This chapter examines what to measure and how to go about doing it. In addition, at the end of this book there is an appendix of free tools an organization can use to jumpstart its measurement program. Here's a look at what is discussed in the rest of the chapter:

Set SMART objectives: Is the measurement program attainable within a reasonable set of guidelines? What are the return on investment and key performance indicators of an organization?

Measure what matters: Since so many things can be measured, it's easy to become distracted. It is crucial to focus on measuring relevant factors.

Use the three A's of online measurement: Action, Attitude and Attention—including in-depth looks at how to measure them.

Setting SMART Objectives

When designing a social media measurement program,

it helps to approach measurement as a discipline. The first step is setting objectives. This is the step where a lion's share of communication and marketing programs (social media or not) fail to perform. It also is where award-winning campaigns shine compared with others. They usually have well-defined objectives, and thus, well-defined results.

Setting objectives is easier with knowledge of what they need to contain. A good place to start is to look through a management lens. The SMART[138] method of setting objectives, which George Doran published in *Management Review*[139] in 1981, calls for specific, measureable, attainable, relevant and time-bound objectives. In other words, the objective should be specified: "how many, by when."

SMART Objectives

S	Specific
M	Measurable
A	Attainable
R	Relevant
T	Time Bound

For example, if an organization runs a social media campaign to support an event, it might write this objective:

"By three months before the event, we will confirm at least 20 online influencers to attend the event, with half of those blogging or otherwise creating content about the event."

The objective is specific in its scope, will allow the organization to see if it is meeting the expected result, is attainable given the time and scope and is relevant to the goal of generating online buzz about the event. The goal is to get at least half of the influencers to create content about it. This is a relational objective, rather than one that will measure sales or a return on investment.

An organization should be sure that objectives support one or more of the key performance indicators (KPIs). [140] KPIs align with the long-term goals of the organization, and, like the SMART objectives, are measureable. An organization may not call them KPIs, but this is a common tool used by management to express the areas in which the organization must perform to succeed.

Talk with the chief financial officer, sales team, owner, executive director or someone of that stature in an organization and ask which numbers are measured regularly. Some KPIs include hard measures—leads and sales for companies, donations for nonprofits and membership for associations. Other KPIs include reducing costs in areas such as customer service or marketing.

For instance, an organization's goal might be to "Be the best place to work in Texas." A helpful KPI would be a low turnover rate. If the social media program is aimed at engaging employees, management might devise a measurement program to look at how many employees engaged with the entity and survey staff members to see if this engagement is affecting their relationship with the organization. To get to outcomes, the organization could look at its turnover rate in relationship to its social networking campaigns, internally or externally, to see if the campaigns had an impact. Also, the organization can track new hires that come through social networking.

As an example of a non-cash KPI, Waste Management invested seed money into a division that it called Greenopolis.

Part of Greenopolis' charter is the goal of reducing solid waste by encouraging recycling. On its community site, Greenopolis[141] has a counter that tracks the tons of glass and aluminum recovered and recycled through its Greenopolis Recycling Kiosk. This is an important KPI for the parent corporation, and it is kept front and center. In late 2010, Waste Management had tracked the recycling of more than 5 million tons through its online efforts.

Certainly there are important softer measures, such as reputation, competitive advantage and key relationships with influencers. Then there are the measures of attention, such as hits, page views, numbers of friends. It isn't that social media is hard to measure—it's that it's hard to decide which of myriad variables are the right ones to measure.

SMART objectives help organizations start from the end and work their way back. In many ways, knowing where a company or nonprofit wants to go creates the strategy and tactics to get there, and the measurement of performance along the way.

Case Study Yahoo! You In?

Yahoo! was looking for a way to more deeply engage its 600 million users to amplify the good works of individuals and embody its brand values of being fun, human, relevant and personal. They also wanted to go beyond supporting a cause—to inspire their base—while also building on the overall goal of their corporate responsibility program to show "How Good Grows."

Yahoo! took an innovative approach by focusing on the stories of average people doing extraordinary things to drive engagement—a case of using content distilled from

---

its user base to drive overall business goals. One example was when a rare Minke whale unexpectedly joined Jodie Nelson as she paddled from Santa Catalina Island to Dana Point for a cancer fundraiser. Yahoo! featured the story on its homepage[142] , and Nelson, who had only raised $6,000 from family and friends, saw that number jump to more than $120,000—all from people donating $20 to $25.

This plays to the core of what Yahoo is trying to inspire with its brand, which is to engage with individuals to make a difference and also move toward its vision, which is to become the center of people's online lives—a hard vision to realize in the fiercely competitive world of search and online media.

Engagement

That was why Yahoo! was in search for something different for its 2009 holiday giving campaign, something that would better highlight its strength as a digital media content and communications provider. It wanted something that would allow its 600 million users to better connect with inspiring ideas and build a stronger emotional bond with the brand. Yahoo! staff drew inspiration from the story of a woman who had impulsively bought groceries for someone at the store; they parlayed that into a fundraising campaign to help others.

Yahoo's "You In?" campaign was conceived as a way to engage the user base by creating a ripple of happiness in social networks. It would start with a simple act of kindness that users could report on their social networks, and particularly in the newly released status update feature in Yahoo! Mail.

Yahoo! seeded the campaign by identifying 300 internal and external influencers and giving them $100 each to perform random acts of kindness. They were to report these acts of kindness in their social networks. The call to action was the tag, "You In?" This encouraged the influencer's social networks to do likewise. The "You In?" reports were added to a Yahoo! map at the website http://kindness.yahoo. com so people could see the impact. Yahoo! took some of the best stories and amplified them with coverage on its dot-com site and also by conducting its own acts of kindness inspired by people's status updates. For instance, inspired by one update, they visited the San Jose airport and paid for luggage fees, resulting in 45 mainstream media articles, just on that one engagement.

Results

The positive results of the "You In?" program extended far beyond the clip books and mainstream media coverage although there was plenty of it. The campaign generated 2,200 mainstream media reports, 1,700 radio mentions and 200 positive mentions on blogs—with one Ad Age headline reading, "Brilliant Holiday Marketing Stunt." This coverage trumped mentions of a concurrent multimillion-dollar ad campaign, a compelling comparison of cost for engagement.

However, perhaps more compelling were the engagement numbers themselves. There were 320,000 status updates from 18 countries, using the Yahoo! Mail status updates feature, an increase in the use of status updates in Yahoo! Mail by 30 percent in a month-to-month comparison. For a media company that bases its income on advertising sales and impressions, it was a tangible business result.

Moreover, the campaign drove 1 million brand impressions for partners Network for Good, Global Giving and Donors Choose, and it resulted in more than $20,000 in donations for nonprofit organizations.[143]

The proof of concept for this program was high, and Yahoo! intends to repeat.[144]

Measuring What Is Important

Once you have decided to measure, the question becomes what to measure. Katie Paine, CEO of measurement firm KDPaine & Partners and author of *Measuring Public Relationships: The Data-Driven Communicator's Guide to Success*,[145] talks about the two laws of measurement: "Only measure that which you can change," and "You become what you measure."

Obviously, an organization should only measure things that matter to it and that it can change, or it is wasting time. Less apparent is that once measurement starts on certain social media activities (like number of friends, for instance), the tendency is to focus on that activity, perhaps to the exclusion of more profitable activities or tactics. There are better sources of measurement than the number of Facebook or Twitter friends. Here are some suggestions for what else to measure and how to get started.

To see how far downhill this thinking can lead, look at recent *New York Times* headline that read: "The Value of a Facebook Friend? About 37 Cents."[146] In a Burger King campaign called the Whopper Sacrifice, users could install a Facebook application, dump 10 friends and get a coupon for a free hamburger. Someone calculated the value of each friend to be about 37 cents by taking the value of a Whopper and dividing it by the number of friends Burger King wanted consumers to drop, yielding the supposed free market value of a friend on Facebook. Of course, not all friends are created equal, and this marketing stunt obviously was not meant to set a value on friends. Unfortunately, however, people do similar things in the measurement of social media every day. Just as arbitrary advertising equivalency values are assigned to coverage in mainstream media to "prove" the worth of an outreach, some social media managers employ the same kind of faulty logic by assigning monetary value to friends, followers and online properties. Resist this urge. Instead, an organization should do what Paine recommends:

> You need to understand what matters to the business [or nonprofit], and how you contribute to that effort. Then you want to measure that, not implement some shiny new object that purports to measure success but in fact is just a proxy for activity or hits or whatever other meaningless number that is out there.[147]

The real question for a company or nonprofit that is using follower counts as its main criterion is, "What do additional Facebook or Twitter friends actually gain us?"

Most likely, the answer isn't clear. The organization needs to focus instead on what those friends do. In a recent study at Northwestern University, Professor Alok Choudhary and graduate student Ramanathan Narayanan found that celebrities with huge followings on Twitter often carry no influence outside their areas of expertise or interest. "Our premise is that influencers are those that dynamically change the opinions of people on specific topics, or the topic of the moment. So in real time we can determine how people are getting influenced for an important topic," said Choudhary. [148]

The Northwestern researchers built an interesting tool called the Pulse of Tweeters[149] that evaluates current Twitter trends based on influence instead of followers, with more action-based measures such as retweets and tonality. While this tool has shortcomings due to its automated nature, it illustrates an important point—that someone with a small, motivated following may be more influential than someone with a vast, but disconnected, following.

Many other tools claim to measure influence, but be wary about using a single, indexed influencer number to measure overall "rank." When it comes to influence, organizations should think bigger.

The value of online followers depends on how an organization engages with them, and on what they do in return. In a post, Augie Ray, a former analyst at Forrester Research, pinpointed the problem of trying to assign value to fans:

> If you lift a ball off the ground and hold it stationary, it has no kinetic energy, but it does have potential energy; drop the ball, and the potential energy becomes kinetic energy.[150] Facebook fans are like that—all potential energy until you introduce something that creates kinetic energy. As such, the operative question isn't, "What is the value of a Facebook Fan?" but "How do I make my Facebook fans valuable?"

Consider how Anas Younes, a doctor at MD Anderson Cancer Center in Houston, Texas, harnessed the power of his fans. Younes specializes in lymphoma and needed more patients to enroll in his clinical trials. For 18 months, he used Twitter and Facebook to share important information about cancer studies and trials, focusing on lymphoma. He amassed a modest but respectable community of 617 followers on his Facebook fan page and 1,511 on Twitter[151] — not bad for a busy doctor, but probably not successful from purely a popularity standpoint.

The key was that his fans were highly motivated by his topic. If someone has lymphoma, Younes is a "go-to" guy. He has built strong thought leadership on Facebook, Twitter and through MD Anderson's Cancerwise blog[152] , and he curates the topic well. As a result, Younes has had a lot of people e-mail him with questions about the disease. More importantly, they are signing up for and referring friends to his clinical trial program. According to Younes, he has quadrupled the number of patients in his clinical trials using social media channels. For a busy doctor who relies on robust participation to further his career, this metric is much more important than the number of Facebook fans he has. Younes has the right fans, who are taking action to benefit his bottom line as a research doctor at a prestigious hospital.

The Three A's of Measurement:
Action. Attitude. Attention.

When it comes to social media measurement, one of the hardest things for most organizations to determine is where to put their limited resources and focus. All measurable objectives for online media should be consolidated to a dashboard that is frequently updated and can show where online efforts stand at a glance.

Dashboard software is available online, but it can be as simple as a PowerPoint document with numbers and goals updated on a monthly basis. Also, entering these numbers into an Excel spreadsheet allows an organization to analyze the numbers for a period of time and to add other data, such as sales numbers.

A word about social media monitoring: It is crucial, and all companies and organizations should invest money and effort into it because it allows them to listen and respond to the Fifth Estate. But monitoring is not, in itself, a measurement program. Analysis of raw monitoring data is necessary to discern what it might mean, or to determine whether there are opportunities to look at data in relationship to other metrics in the organization. A measurement program starts with monitoring, but it requires more than looking at the number of mentions of a brand, organization or issue.

Types of measurement include three gauges: Attention, Attitude and Action . These roughly correspond to the more traditional measures of communication: Outcomes, Outtakes and Outputs, which gained popularity with researchers in 2002.[153]

Measuring Action

Probably the most important and least measured part of a social media campaign is the action people take as a result.

This is where campaigns can be tied to key performance indicators (KPIs) or other organizational goals for action. Return on investment also can be measured in terms of actions.

Business measures can include things such as registrations for conferences, sales leads, hiring, store traffic and reduction in customer service costs. For nonprofits, business goals include donations, votes (for politicians), new volunteers, return volunteers, volume of donations and the median amount of money per donation.

One useful example is a research study conducted by Altimeter and WetPaint called EngagementdB[154], which sought to connect key business results to social media engagement. The study looked at the engagement in social media by 100 top brands as measured by *BusinessWeek* / Interbrand "Best Global Brands 2008" rankings and correlated that engagement with one of the biggest KPIs for many organizations—revenue and profit.

The study found brands that were highly engaged in a number of social media and networking channels showed stronger revenue and profit than those that were not. Moreover, it found that those that were not active in social networking performed worse in all categories than those that were. The correlation is striking, because it indicates the need for an open mindset of listening and responding to the needs of customers, donors or other stakeholders for a company or organization to be successful.

In his "Basics of Social Media ROI"[155] presentation, Olivier Blanchard, author of *Social Media ROI,* outlines a process to tie social media activities to revenue and cost savings that includes looking at sales data overlaid with social media activities and campaigns. He recommends looking at frequency, or number of transactions per month; reach, or number of new customers; and yield, or total transactions.

For example, overlay basic sales data with social media activities, the results of your monitoring and any market research, then look at the data for areas where they seem to rise in concert (commonly known as deltas in the measurement world). This kind of measurement is best done for a significant period of time to give the best results, and it can demonstrate which social media activities and campaigns appear to be having the best effect.

If an organization noticed that more lively chatter on its Facebook page usually means better attendance at weekend events, it might consider timing communication or promotions for maximum effectiveness. Determine what's most important to the business, and start measuring that right away. More variables can always be added, and it's better to start small than not to start at all.

Universe of social media measurement includes:

• KPIs, with SMART objectives that map to them

• Monitoring mentions of the organization and looking at the balance of positive, negative and neutral mentions

• Analytics, including number of comments, unique users, popular content, time spent on page

• Business data, sales, volume and other raw data that can be correlated to activities

• Market research, including satisfaction survey results and pre- and post-attitudinal studies

• Chart of activities, to link them back to data points

Case Study: Fire Nancy Pelosi

After the 2008 election, the Republican Party (or the "Grand Old Party," the GOP), invested extensively in its social media capabilities. In its efforts, the GOP took on a participation and crowdsource strategy, building a core group of followers who support the party and its platforms. In addition to primary tools Facebook and Twitter, the GOP hired Todd Herman to direct their online effort, community managers, and developers. This team tools an open API to integrate the social effort into the electronic database maintained by the Republican National Committee.

By the time the 2010 general election began in earnest, the GOP had developed a large constituency, far surpassing the reach of a Republican newspaper in a major market like the *Washington Times*. The GOP had embraced and become a part of the Fifth Estate. This social media power was unleashed after the health-care reform act was passed by the U.S. Congress. In response, the Republicans launched a "Fire Nancy Pelosi" campaign to galvanize their core nationally and change the balance of power in Congress.

Engagement

When it became clear that Congress was going to move health-care reform through, the Republicans developed their response. They integrated their Fifth Estate engagement using the firenancypeosi.com domain, the new GOP.com, Facebook, Twitter, the Points API key for "Fire Pelosi" donation widgets and—most importantly—their influencers.

Before officially launching the Pelosi campaign, the GOP reached out to its core 100 influencers. A hashtag keyword—#firepelosi—was created for use on Twitter to track conversations via search and encourage other like minded individuals to participate too. #firepelosi started to appear early because the party seeded it. Then the campaign began in earnest with a TweetBomb and the GOP unleashing its full community on the effort. "Fire Nancy Pelosi" became a Twitter-driven phenomenon, trending on the social network for a day because so many people were posting #firepelosi tweets.

Then Twitter drove widget adoption, which linked back to the Fire Pelosi website and drove search results. The fresh content on Fire Pelosi drove it to become the third-highest link anytime someone searched the name "Nancy Pelosi." After Google searches (achieved organically by the high number of Twitter mentions) sustained the campaign, the GOP turned to Facebook community members and asked for donations. Donations on Facebook cascaded via up-dates, galvanizing friend networks to follow suit and make their own donations.

Results

The Republican Party experienced a 100-to-1 return on investment, spending $17,000 to raise $1.7 million via the FireNancyPelosi.com widgets and donation tools. Perhaps even more amazing was the 22,800 widgets that were distributed, customized for each blogger or content owner's site.

An even more incredible telltale sign was the size of some of the donations. Often criticized for being a medium that doesn't deliver big donations, the Republican social media effort provided a different result. The GOP received eight donations of $16,200, the federal cap for a political donation from an individual. When the GOP won 60 Congressional seats in the 2010 mid-term election, the Fire Pelosi campaign was credited by several media outlets as starting the inertia that led to the groundswell election.

Measuring the "Three Ss" of Attitude

In addition to knowing how and why people in the Fifth Estate take action, measurement can help an organization know how they feel about an organization or brand. Attitudes provide an idea of a person's relationship to a brand or issue. The "Three Ss" of attitudes measure this attribute: Sentiment, Satisfaction and Surveying.

Sentiment is an important way to gauge the attitude of people in the Fifth Estate toward an organization and to get a "feel for the conversation." Organizations can use this data to "read the tea leaves" and make wiser decisions to better manage the expectations of a community. It's possible to measure sentiment using free tools that collect the raw data and analyze the sentiment. Paid services also can prepare this data. Usually, the category buckets for sorting this data are positive, negative and neutral.

An organization, topic or brand with large volume will want to consider using a paid tool. Many of these tools apply an automatic sentiment score to the data feed; but some measurement professionals say that this figure can be off-target by as much as 70 percent. While monitoring tools such as Radian6, Spiral16, Sysomo, Social Media Metrics and myriad others are useful for gathering large amounts of data, there still is a need to define what falls into the positive, negative and neutral sentiment buckets. This requires a human to make sure articles and posts are tabulated correctly.

For instance, if someone said, "I had a hell of a time at the opening of the show," a computer might put that in a negative bucket, while any human would know immediately that the commenter loved the show. Then there is the problem of spam. All paid services work hard to filter it out, but usually a significant amount of spam gets classified into one of the three buckets—enough to make a real difference. A person needs to look at each entry (or at a sample of entries) and make judgment calls.[156]

Sentiment is a great measure when done right, and it can be especially useful when overall sentiment is compared with that of competitors. It also helps show that online activities, such as providing customer service through Twitter or engaging a negative community, are helping improve a company's reputation.

The second "S" is old-fashioned satisfaction. When it comes to social media measurement, people sometimes forget to use what already is at their disposal. A customer-focused organization typically asks people about their satisfaction after a sale. It can take these scores and add some questions about customer engagement in social media channels. Then measurement is as easy as cross-tabulating satisfaction scores with the level of social network interaction.

If an organization does not offer a consumer product, it still can gauge the satisfaction of visitors to its blog or website by using a pop-up exit survey. According to analytics guru Avinash Kaushik,[157] there are three questions an organization should ask on any website survey of its customers:

1. What is the purpose of your visit to our website today?
2. Were you able to complete your task?
3. If you were not able to complete your task, why not?

These questions give insight into why people came to the blog or website and whether they were able to complete their purpose for being there. If people routinely can't complete tasks, an organization can learn what is frustrating them and work to fix it.

The third "S" is a "survey of relationship." In the paper, "Guidelines for Measuring Relationships in Public Relations," Linda Childers Hon and James E. Grunig lay out a series of questions that gives an immediate snapshot of what is working and what isn't in the relationship with key online stakeholders and gives insights into how to improve it. [158]

Use simple pre- and post-surveys to see how attitudes have shifted because of a campaign or program. Also use online focus groups to test new ideas, get feedback on product development and avoid pitfalls in social media outreach. In measuring attitudes, organizations have to take the old-fashioned approach of talking to people rather than relying heavily on computer-generated insights.

How to Measure Attention

Attention is perhaps the most measured aspect of social networks. Often the counts of followers, "likes," links, comments and perhaps retweets and mentions are the only form of measurement to which the organization pays attention. But these measures are inadequate. They can be gamed[159] by determined people hoping to gain influence, and they tell very little about what people are doing in relation to a brand.

Respected people in the online media and technology community have raised questions about the efficacy of this measurement strategy. Iain McDonald of Amnesia RazorFish in Australia wrote a detailed post[160] on how to spot when someone has been gaming the system, and blogger and influencer Anil Dash[161] has pointed out the problem with Twitter accounts that amass a passive following that wasn't earned through merit. Dash observed that these accounts do not experience a commensurate growth in engagement as their follower counts skyrocket.

The issue of gaming aside, an organization probably knows very little about those who follow its social media accounts. Are they competitors, spambots, friends or foes? Can the organization discern the difference? Aliza Sherman, blogger at the popular tech blog GigaOm[162] argues for seeking quality followers rather than quantity. Remember lymphoma specialist Anes Younes? He had the right followers to meet his objectives. That is what a company or nonprofit needs: quality interactions (retweets, mentions, clicks on links, comments) in its community.

However, interaction numbers tell very little about why the interest was generated. Increased traffic to a blog could mean that people really love the most recent post, or it could mean that the search engine indexed the page for an irrelevant search term. For instance, a post about the marketing strategy of entertainment phenomenon Justin Bieber could garner hundreds of hits from teens looking for the latest Bieber news rather than from potential customers. An analytics tool for keyword search traffic would show entry via the term "Justin Bieber," and a corresponding, atypical spike in the average number of "bounces" (people who come to the site, read one page and leave) would indicate the traffic is useless to the organization.

Blog analytics can be thought of as content, relationships and action. Look at how content is performing, what an audience finds most interesting, where they are spending their time and how loyal they are to the blog. Some of the most interesting analytics reports on a blog include the content overview, which can help to set the editorial calendar; the number of absolute unique visitors, which is much more accurate than hits or traffic; and the number of return vs. new visitors, which shows readers' loyalty.

On a social website or blog, a high bounce rate is less problematic because many readers come from a link on another social site or feedreader and leave after reading. However, time spent on the site might be a good measure to watch, and knowing which content is more compelling allows an organization to tweak popular pages to get more engagement and more click-throughs.

Measuring relationships in an analytics program is a bit harder. Traffic sources can be a telling sign. Return visitors, top traffic referrals and the average time people spend on the blog site are some of the standard analytics that merit the most attention. For instance, by knowing which sites share information and send traffic to a site, a community manager can encourage or reward the people behind those posts by acknowledging them. Moreover, an organization can test how blog posts are generating action by using unique links to e-commerce, donation or other action pages. In the free program Google Analytics, this kind of link is called a "tag," and these links can be used to follow the reader from the blog content all the way to the sale.[163]

More than anything else, keywords should drive an organization's search engine optimization strategy. This is achieved by looking at the keywords people are using to find a site and then modifying copy to bring in more qualified traffic. If certain keywords are performing well in both overall traffic and stickiness—meaning lots of people are staying on the page long enough to read the content—then an organization has likely found its natural audience. Cater to them to drive up the relational measure of return visitors, or loyalty.

The most loyal fans deserve red-carpet treatment. Give them content that interests them. If a small core of people returns every week to spend a significant amount of time on the site, be sure to work at growing this segment by providing them more of the content that interests them. Growing a community includes increasing unique visitors, return visitors, time spent on site and number of pages viewed.

Becoming a Measurement Maven

Effective social media measurement is not nearly as difficult as the "Naysayers" believe. Nor is it as complicated as the "Bean Counters" would like it to be. Professionals who learn how to take the universe of measurable information and parse it into actionable insights that can drive strategy will have the best chance of success. Just because something can be measured doesn't mean it should be, and just because "everyone else" is valuing a particular measure doesn't mean it is right for every organization.

It is important to measure that which is central to the overall goal of the organization. If that is sales, it's important to correlate them with customer/follower relationships, because those can be the basis for future sales. Determine if the growth of relationships helps drive sales higher. If the important measure is increased volunteers, measure how social media participation tracks against volunteerism and survey volunteers to see if an organization's social media-based volunteers differ from those who don't use conversational media.

CHAPTER SIX SNAPSHOTS

Like many forms of communication, social media can be difficult to measure. There are three views of social media measurement, the Naysayers who believe that social media shouldn't be measured because it's about people; the Bean Counters who don't believe social media should be engaged in unless they produce hard results, and the Explorers who look at a variety of measurements.

Measurement not only displays results, but also can serve as a diagnostic tool. By determining whether or not a program is succeeding in its goals, changes can be made and adjustments can occur, furthering the organization's business or advocacy goals.

Set SMART Objectives

SMART objectives are specific, measurable, attainable, relevant and time-bound. An organization can use these guidelines to frame the parameters of online measurement, from hard sales numbers to the speed of interaction.

Measure What Matters

Industry thought leader Katie Paine says, "Only measure that which you can change," and, "You become what you measure." That does not include Twitter and Facebook follower accounts. Organizations need to do more than just look at the numbers. They have to determine what these numbers mean to their business or cause.

Measure Action

Measuring action provides the hard data. It's here that an organization determines which online social efforts are driving results. Facebook posts that yield sales and social media programs that create stronger loyalty and retention are examples of actions.

Measuring Attitude

Attitude is how people feel about the organization. Given that social media are relational, it's easy to measure the emotional ties to an organization (or lack thereof). To measure attitude, use the three "Ss," sentiment, satisfaction and surveying.

Measuring Attention

Attention, follower counts, number of posts, tweets, etc., are the most popular kind of social media measurement online. It's important to tie these measurements to actions that are drawing attention, so that an organization can maximize these activities and optimize its online program. Further, measuring attention enables the empowerment of the organization's loyal influencers.

Chapter 7

Sustaining Your Community Over Time

Care2 is a community comprising 15 million people interested in societal issues around all sorts of change, from climate issues to human rights. In an online conversation, Founder and CEO Randy Paynter discussed how important it is to stay relevant after ten years as an online community developer, and how your interactions need to change over time to continue to foster growth.[164] Maintaining position online is one of the biggest challenges facing organizations now that their initial forays into online media have matured. Once you have developed a following, moving from a conversation driver to a conversation facilitator is crucial. It empowers the community to become part of the brand, as Paynter noted.

That's why Dell's social effort continues to thrive after its difficult "Dell Hell" turnaround in 2006 and 2007. That turnaround featured an online reputation nightmare with almost half of all posts about Dell featuring a negative tone, and catchphrase—Dell Hell—that was associated with its customer service. Dell reduced negative commentary by more than half through active listening and direct engagement, resolving Internet users concerns, case by case.

The company keeps innovating and responding, externally and internally, to its community. In 2010, Dell began systematically training every employee, to use social media tools in their job,s facilitating better communications in every aspect of Dell's business. The company culture has become truly social.

Dell is the unusual case. More often brands suffer from "one-hit wonder" success. The summer of 2010 saw a viral hit with the "Old Spice Guy," a series of advertisements mixed with social media that featured a buff, shirtless actor addressing witty quips about manliness to the ladies in his audience. The Internet was awash in buzz and discussion among people eager to get a response from the Old Spice Guy in video or on Twitter.[165] By autumn, the concept was aging, and the buzz started dying down. Old Spice switched to an ad campaign with football spokespersons, targeted toward men.

Just as community behaviors change, online technologies rapidly evolve New features develop, social networks are born and others fade into obscurity. Communities adapt and move in and out of social networks quickly over time.

Maintaining relevance requires a "think liquid" attitude that allows your organization to move with the times and serve your stakeholders. Like flowing water, which finds the path of least resistance to the ocean, an organization needs to remain flexible and follow its community—using the tools that it finds most relevant in the moment. Can you imagine if your favorite nonprofits and brands still insisted on using AOL?[166]

One of the reasons Facebook and Twitter remain relevant is that they are constantly, proactively upgrading their feature to serve the people using their networks. While the networks came to prominence in 2007, in 2010 just last year they both underwent major adaptation–Facebook with its "Like" technology, and Twitter with its first major interface change since its launch. When presenting video and pictorial content becomes more important, these services focus on them. If shareability needs to be optimized, the networks adapt.

Like technologies, issues stay in motion, too. If a brand or nonprofit is too rigid in its methods of staying on topic or message, it may miss the boat. Plus, an organization can become comfortable repeating a successful conversation.

Dictating interesting points of view to the Fifth Estate may capture its attention, but if there's no give and take, no commitment to serving the community's evolving interests, it will move on. Common interest is a two-way street.

Because the Fifth Estate represents a wide swath of our society's voices—real people—it changes. Relevance to our various communities is about a commitment to changing and evolving with the times.

Organizations that have had success within their social communities might feel like they have mastered the crowd. That's an easy trap to fall into. People—particularly those who comprise the vociferous Fifth Estate—are complex. No one person has a singular area of interest. People like or don't like the arts, sports, civic activity, working, parenting, family, etc.

For an organization to assume it can capture their interest and maintain it is short-sighted.

In reality, the Fifth Estate may become aligned with an organization for a period of time, then move on. As Charlene Li and Josh Bernoff note throughout their book *Groundswell,* the community's support can rise and fall in a moment.[167] Engaging interested Fifth Estate members in a conversation about a cause or a company's products and services over a long period of time is extraordinarily difficult.

American interest in organizations is transitory. In the United States, more than 2.5 million charities compete for volunteers.[168] According to the National Conference on Citizenship, 62 million Americans volunteered with a nonprofit between 2007 and 2009.[169] Yet, 18.6 million people took action with their neighbors independent of a 501(c)(3) to fix a community problem. That's 29% of the larger 501(c)(3) volunteer base. Even with an overcrowded nonprofit sector, causes cannot capture all of the actions Americans engage in, and in fact, they miss many opportunities to serve as vehicles volunteerism.

In the 2009 movie "Up in the Air," George Clooney as Ryan Bingham said, "There's nothing cheap about loyalty." Getting, and then keeping, a community engaged requires dedication and a commitment to serve, with an eye on moving with the community's technological choices and interests. The rest of this chapter discusses several key tenets of sustaining long-term communities online:

- Social network agnosticism (The Death of Facebook)
- Mobility as the next Thing
- Attitudes toward Technology evolution

- Evolving community management
- Changing influence

Case Study: Dell Becomes a Social Enterprise

Dell was one of the first big breakthroughs using social media. During a period of time in 2006 and 2007, the company engaged in a customer service program to turn around its reputation. It started with a 49 percent negative blog post ratio and reduced overall tonality to 22 percent negative.

As the program evolved, it launched the successful Direct2Dell blog, a series of secondary support blogs and community sites like the crowdsourcing IdeaStorm. In the years since 2007, more than 400 ideas submitted on IdeaStorm have become actual product ideas.

Now after years of success, the company is trying adopt social media as a tool across the whole fabric of the company, toward building better business, not just better communication.

The company sees social media as a great tool, and it is attempting to embrace it as a betterment measure across the entire organization, in effect becoming a "socialprise."

"This is not about campaigns or initiatives," said Richard Binhammer, senior manager for outreach communications and executive initiatives, social media and community at Dell. "It's about adopting social media as a way to do better business."

Engagement

Dell's social revitalization began in earnest during late 2010. To achieve its objectives, practically every social media tool has been deployed internally. The organization blogs. It uses a crowdsourcing site employeestorm, mirroring its popular consumer effort IdeaStorm; it uses (chatter a micro blogging platform like Twitter).

To help the organization adapt, Dell has robust training initiatives with employee conferences in each of its global regions, as well as training programs that lead to certification as social media and community professionals. At the time of writing, more than 2,000 people had been trained in the space of two months. In addition to certification, Dell has been training employees across the enterprise on the use of listening and conversation tools.

Results

A daily tracking report is e-mailed to more than 500 people (including the CEO, CMO and lead of each business unit) in the organization highlighting top topics in social media and overall Twitter reach of various conversation threads. Interest in adoption is high across the organization.

"I can tell you that our four major business units—enterprise, public sector, small and medium business, as well as consumer—all seem to be adopting social media as a viable tool ... to use and connect directly with customers," Binhammer said. "Our product group is also engaging both on and off of dell.com."

Early signs are positive, with increased visits to Dell. com, sentiment, share of voice, revenue generated. Binhammer promises more statistics will come in 2011.

The Death of Facebook

Who in their right mind would predict the death of Facebook, given its ever-increasing dominance?[170] But everyone always asks, "What's next?"

One thing long-term Internet citizens have seen over the past 30 years: communities and social networks get large, even as dominant as Facebook now is, and then they fade. Some stay relevant as leaders in their niches—YouTube, for example—and others drop into a second tier, or worse. Friendster, MySpace and AOL exist in some form to this day, but none of them enjoys the leadership positions and mindshare of their heyday.

One of the secrets to Facebook's longevity is its replication of the McDonald's business model. McDonald's offers a cheap menu of foods and beverages that contemporary society demands. If a customer wants a latte, they can go to McDonald's. Ice cream? McDonald's offers soft serve. Salad? No problem! And McDonald's still offers the now classic Big Mac, just in case someone wants a burger.

Facebook does the same with its social network functionality. It literally watches competitors create new features, and then it incorporates those functionalities into its network, competing head-to-head in that functional space. Facebook relies on its incredibly large user base to accept and use the new features. We saw this with Facebook Places and the competition it offers Foursquare. Other examples include:

- Facebook Pictures competes with Flickr
- Facebook Video competes with YouTube (this feature does as well as a McRib sandwich on market share)
- Facebook Chat competes with AOL's AIM
- Facebook Questions and Groups, compete with LinkedIn Questions and Groups

One could argue that the strength of this business model is also Facebook's weakness. As we have seen over time, Facebook constantly updates its interface to incorporate these changes. This is relatively easy because of its text-based, three-column layout. While text allows Facebook to offer all of these features, the user interface has become junky and cumbersome. In essence, being the McDonald's of social networks has forced it into an over-reliance on text.

If a competing technology arose that provided a new interface, an almost completely visual tactile (touch) input to a social application, then Facebook would be challenged to completely redesign its web site. Several new apps on iPad have shown a new way to interact. Early signs show these applications are becoming immensely popular.

One iPad application, Flipboard, allows users to create their own magazines based on preferences and socially recommended content. ABC's popular iPad app features a visual globe of news stories. Both application interfaces rely heavily on pictures with very few words, and why shouldn't they, given that a picture is worth a thousand words?

It's only a question of time—maybe even within the next two years—before a primarily visual-interface-based social network launches. Processing time, software development and bandwidth inevitably will increase to enable it.

How will Facebook upgrade its interface to compete with this kind of innovation?

It would take an almost complete gutting of its social networking code. Facebook's system has become so clunky that Facebook CEO Marc Zuckerberg can't make changes that he wants to in order to open the network. Plus Facebook's original feature of private, closed social networking was its big differentiator. The privacy tension caused by the movement toward openness continues to haunt Facebook.[171]

Such a network upgrade likely would force Facebook to

abandon users who are still text-based. It would be very hard for McDonald's to keep serving Big Macs while offering a tastier Filet Mignon sandwich that holds market share (Angus Wraps aside). If you think Facebook cannot unseated,or it will not be by a tactile-input-based network, what about a video-based network? Bandwidth and technology permitting, how about Third Life, a better version of Second Life's would-be virtual-avatar-based world, where interaction would occur in a computer-generated 3-D environment? Or a video-based network like, but more nimble than, the original Seesmic?

Isn't it just a question of time before Facebook meets a competitor with a better, next-generation interface that it can't match? Yes given the context of Internet history and technology development.

If a better, easier choice becomes available, you can expect people to spend more time on it than on Facebook. The Fifth Estate moves with what's hot, and without thinking about the historical value of today's technology platform of choice.

Business leaders and strategists cannot afford to become too entrenched on a mega social network like Facebook or Twitter. If an organization cannot move with its community because of an over-investment in one network, it loses the opportunity to serve stakeholders effectively.

Mobility As the Next Thing

If one had to read the sands of time to find the next big evolution in online media, they wouldn't have to look far. According to Pew Internet, in 2010 40% of adults use the Internet, e-mail or instant messaging on a mobile phone (up from the 32% of Americans who did this in 2009).[172] Of that group, 38% browse the Web using their phones.

This trend, in combination with the ever-growing (and cheaper) smartphone marketplace, represents the greatest sea change on the social web since Facebook opened its firewalls to welcome members who were not enrolled in universities.[173] Positioning a company or nonprofit to effectively engage stakeholders on their smartphones, tablets or other portable devices only makes sense. Mobility is the most obvious change that communities are making wholesale on the Internet.

Mobile web access is expected to surpass desktop access by 2014.[174] Because of the wide proliferation of mobile phone platforms — iPhones, Android, Blackberries, Windows — it makes the most sense to develop your site to, at minimum, offer a great mobile experience before considering any particular application. Applications can be costly, only work on singular platforms (iPhone, Android, Blackberry, etc.), and need to offer more value than simply repackaged Web content.

Beyond the obvious mobile Web come usage changes in patterns and how they affect the data and user. There are many questions here spurred by the location-based social network craze—with Foursquare and Gowalla taking the lead and Facebook and Twitter trying to compete. However, experts are beginning to notice that check-in programs do not offer real long-term value for organizations.[175]

The real development is in understanding how people use their phones to engage the Web, and then building mobile programs to serve the customer. In some cases, that may mean delving into a location-based social network's database via its API and developing custom applications or unique information to serve the community.

Consider that Central Park is the most checked-in place in New York City on location-based network Foursquare.[176] Central Park supported this latent community by adding historical data for check-ins throughout the park, providing context and information to the average Foursquare/Central Park visitor's experience. There also are mobile applications that let people track where they are in the park and find attractions and locations near them.

Understanding how mobile data can benefit your stakeholder is the key. [Whether that's easier experiences with less input because of touch interfaces, or actual hard location-based use depends on the organization.] What is clear is that this is a trend that companies and nonprofits can no longer avoid.

Attitudes Toward Technology Evolution

Evolving technology and revelant conversations are crucial to the lifeblood of any community. Balancing the two—serving community and adapting new tools—always revolves around two principles: A relentless focus on the community's actual use of technology and consistent willingness to experiment.

A crucial component to success is ensuring that an organization's evolution in social media adheres to its community's needs and purpose. That means serving the community with valuable content, tools and conversations that are on-topic and on-mission.

Adopting new tools that better serve the community is a

constant consideration and an exercise in experimentation and testing. Sometimes that means moving away from a technology or application that's becoming universal because it is not well used by a specific community. In other cases, it may mean focusing on popular older tools. Technology adoption requires serving the community with valuable content, tools and conversations that all seek to sustain momentum. The meme "serving to sustain" is ever-present, regardless of tactic or approach.

To illustrate the universality of serving to sustain, I conducted qualitative research with Care2, Dell, the Humane Society of the United States, LinkedIn and Wiser Earth.[177] Their disparate goals include one providing professionals with vast social networking capabilities; one dedicated to a social network community focused on change of all kinds; a smaller social network that works to build a sustainable ethos; a major cause whose community is network-agnostic and focuses on animal rights; and Dell's IdeaStorm, a community crowdsourcing site that has created more than 400 product ideas for the computer manufacturer.

In the cases of Care2 and LinkedIn, their communities are a decade old and existed well before the rise of Twitter and Facebook. The Humane Society, Dell's IdeaStorm and Wiser Earth are newer, with their social efforts started in 2006 or 2007. All five have kept their communities engaged.

Whether it was continuously adapting to the community's changing technology needs, a relentless focus on mission, or empowering access and information exchange through larger networks, these social networks and communities—while completely different in scope and scale—have done what was necessary to survive and prosper. Here's a glimpse at some of the common methods they share.

LinkedIn has a unique technology approach, investing in new products and data analytics, so that professionals can more easily find one another, connect and discuss topics they care about. Technology and feature adoption always revolves around this mission. Perhaps the greatest example of this is its groups feature set, which at the time of writing had 600,000 groups, with 1,000 groups added every day and 100,000 professionals joining a group every day. Other examples include its People You May Know service and its new popular Company Profiles.

The Humane Society's team of six community managers is challenged by what could be called consistent platform flux. They continue to adapt their approach on networks like Facebook as the networks evolve, in turn producing new community behaviors. For example, as Facebook newsfeeds become flooded with branded messaging, it becomes more important to be selective in the organization's communications. In addition, the team is always experimenting with the latest tools to see which ones the community adapts to. This includes participating, creating contests and experimenting with geo-location tools.

During the first year of Dell's IdeaStorm in 2007, its operation continually evolved based on community feedback. Three years later in 2010, Dell began considering how best to revitalize IdeaStorm. To ensure that it serves the community, the company is conducting conversations that will determine its future direction.

For example, Dell community members may suggest a

relevant idea, but because a product that would use the concept has just been launched, the company ends up tabling it for months. For the new IdeaStorm, Dell has beta-tested a feature called "storm sessions." This rapid conversation topic is for a short, defined period and seeks specific feedback related to a particular business matter under consideration. This is being considered as potential solution to the time-alignment problem between product launches and idea suggestions.

Care2 involves its community in its technology evolution decisions, going to great depths to ensure that there are no surprises when a feature set is unleashed. The network deploys surveys, listens to feedback and analyzes use data before making product decisions. Then it solicits feedback before making significant site changes. Wiser Earth management also pays close attention to its community and polls its members for feedback on new features.

Integrating Major Social Networks

To not use the behemaths of major social networks is to deny one's effort access to the larger Fifth Estate. General networks like Twitter and Facebook serve as beachheads to participate in larger community conversations. By engaging in these networks, an organization can draw interested parties into more specific community conversations.

On the opposite side of the spectrum, community members rarely limit their conversation to one network or one topic. Empowering fluid conversation out of specific community conversations only makes sense.

Both Care2 and Wiser Earth integrated Facebook and Twitter connectivity as those networks rose to prominence.

Wiser Earth opened WiserEarth's directory through an API in a campaign called OpenWiser, and its Executive Director Peggy Duvette runs their Twitter presence. Care2 deployed community managers operating on Facebook and Twitter, added its petition functionality as an application on Facebook and integrated StumbleUpon into its offering.

Although LinkedIn is more of a direct, professional-oriented competitor to Facebook, it, too, integrated Twitter capabilities into its status update offering. This created a popular feature that turns LinkedIn updates into tweets and turns professional tweets into status posts using the #in hashtag.

The Humane Society also plays on both networks, But the organization is mindful that things can change. "It's important to not focus on the technology, but on the people," said Carie Lewis, the organization's director of emerging media. "Build a loyal community so if Facebook disappears, and you're forced to go somewhere else, they will follow." Dell also has integrated Facebook into IdeaStorm.

Evolving Community Management

When a community development effort begins, it often requires significant amounts of effort, from participation and relationship development to content creation and seeding "influentials" with ideas. While to some extent these efforts never stop, part of sustaining a community is letting the community run itself.

Consider the dynamics of a great party. For it to be truly memorable, usually the host of the party must be gracious and allow the guests to mingle, discovering each other and the commonalities they may share. The host, while obviously playing a central role, doesn't dominate the party, but rather acts as facilitator—seeding the gathering with libations and merriment.

Applying that philosophy to online communities, an organization needs to embrace the Fifth Estate's independence and empower individual members to become active leaders in a community. Organizations need to encourage continued participation by celebrating input and giving it a central role in the facilitated conversation. That sometimes means that topics and features are developed to meet the community's actual conversation.

Going back to a few of the case studies from the previous section on technology, Wiser Earth develops new content areas and promotes volunteers who want to be active as editors. When climate talks became a dominant conversation topic in the community, Wiser Earth created a group for live reports from Copenhagen.

Care2 takes the approach of building larger networks that facilitate conversations and connectivity, and it generally focuses on tools that support those conversations. While laissez-faire in its community management, Care2 found that its blog content was encouraging more community participation than its groups were. In response, it developed channels of content dedicated to areas of change so its participants would have more opportunity to converse in greater depth and specifics.

In addition to action on the behalf of animal rights, the Humane Society uses its social tools to encourage fun conversations about pets. While one could argue this has nothing to do with taking action, it does empower community members to feel like they belong to a larger group of like-minded animal lovers.

Keeping the Peace

It is crucial to be extremely sensitive to a community's needs and foibles. Communities, whether they are tens of millions of people or hundreds of thousands, are painstaking about contact and behavior so they thrive. This includes building in mechanisms to minimize disruption and to ensure that the larger mission is accomplished.

For example, the Humane Society limits the amount of "asks" it makes, so when it does reach out to community members, it is taken seriously. LinkedIn lubricates more connectivity and interaction by providing a "clean, well-lit venue." Dell manages IdeaStorm with an eye toward maintaining an active flow of ideas and aligning ideas from the community with its own products.

If the larger community's interests are to be encouraged and sustained, than community-centric behavior needs to be enforced. That means the organization will have to use some of its community management resources to enforce and even build new rules.

Care2 deploys community managers who artfully work through conflicts to ensure that passionate conversations about change don't devolve into painful personality conflicts. Wiser Earth had to develop a clear governance structure that applied to volunteers, partners, board and staff.

This can be particularly true of crowdsourcing initiatives. While the crowd craves freedom, people need to be told how to participate and what the rules of engagement are. These rules have to be clear, empowering of the crowd and directive in their end result. Unfortunately, even with rules in place, community "policing" can become necessary. Rules can be broken, the spirit of a contest can be thwarted and unforeseen behaviors can necessitate action.[178]

Perhaps the largest crowdsourcing effort in history, the Pepsi Refresh project, seeks input from the general American public on great ideas that need funding to benefit local communities. The beverage company needed to adjust its official rules in June 2010 to address fraudulent voting that was taking place. People were using bots or software programs to auto-vote as a proxy. Further, the project management team continuously monitors the community to ensure that the rules are being followed, quality levels are up to par and votes are indeed authentic.

"Throughout the duration of the program, we've worked with a number of organizations that ensure that voting processes adhere to the rules, grants are implemented according to budget and timelines, and we have a team that works each day to respond to consumer inquiries," said Shiv Singh, head of digital for PepsiCo Beverages. "In addition, a member of the Pepsi organization reviews every one of the thousand submissions each month to ensure the quality of ideas on the refresheverything.com site."[179]

Case Study: charity: water

One of the more popular brands in nonprofit social media has been charity: water. From its appearance as a favorite among bloggers to its designation as beneficiary for the first Twestival, charity: water remains present. As social media has evolved, so have charity: water's efforts,

---

demonstrating a brand that can sustain and build upon its community. This was reaffirmed with its September 2010 birthday campaign.

In 2006, founder Scott Harrison "gave up" his September birthday party and raised enough money to build six wells in Uganda. In 2007, more people joined in and raised $150,000 to provide water projects in Kenya. The 2008 campaign saw charity: water focus on Ethiopia and raise $1 million. In 2009, the social-media-integrated mycharitywater platform was launched to enable grassroots fundraising for anyone supporting the cause. In 13 months, that site raised more than $4 million.

In September 2010, charity: water focused on Central African Republic, one of the poorest countries in the world. The key goals: bring clean and safe drinking water to all 16,000 Bayaka people who don't have access to clean water, and to provide all of them with the necessary access to fund solutions that would bring clean water to 90,000 people through 210 water projects. The goal is to raise $1.7 million—all of it online, and the vast majority of it via individual fundraising campaigns on mycharitywater.

Engagement

The organization used several social media channels and tools to engage stakeholders:
- Vimeo to share video footage
- Facebook to connect with the audience
- Custom "September" tab with quiz, gifts, etc.
- Twitter to connect with charity: water's community

In addition to social media, charity: water deployed a larger, integrated campaign. Elements included e-mail marketing, outreach to influential figures and celebrities, a full media and search plan provided pro bono by Razorfish and pro bono PR support to pitch bloggers and traditional media from Golin Harris.

The average fundraiser on mycharitywater raises $1,000, so the organization targeted at least 2,000 campaigners. The greatest point of connection was a "Live Drill" on Sept. 7, 2010, in Moale, an isolated village that has never had clean water and seen attempted wells fail twice in the past 20 years. Unfortunately, the charity: water well also failed. But the cause shared the story, and the community responded with resolve. As charity: water moved to a nearby village to try again, the community rallied, and the first successful well of the September campaign was drilled.[180]

Results

September was charity: water's most successful month ever in terms of money raised on mycharitywater.org and traffic to the site, significantly outshining any other month in the cause's history. By early October, the 2010 effort started with a large surge, totaling $720,901 raised, 100 percent online via mycharitywater.org by grassroots individual fundraisers in all, 2,040 people started September campaigns between Aug. 16 and Sept. 30, 2010, to raise money for the Central African Republic.

Grassroots fundraisers varied from celebrities to communities, as well as beneficiaries. Will and Jada Smith joined the fight and gave up their September birthdays and raised more than $60,000. The Ruby on Rails programming community raised more than $37,000: Tariku, a child adopted from Ethiopia who lost a brother to waterborne disease, raised more than $5,000.

"Core brand attributes make it easy for us to play in social media," said Paull Young, director of digital media for charity: water. "Our 100% model means we send every dollar donated to the field, making us true partners with our donors. Trust: We 'prove' our projects by marking each water project on Google Maps and showing our donors where their individual money went. Transparency: We're

> not afraid to 'fail' as shown by our live drill. Our greatest commitment is to our fundraisers, we're much more focused on working with our supporters to help them raise money for us, than in repeatedly asking them for money or trying to drive clicks on a donate button."

Changing Influence

Sometimes at events, I like to sit in the back row. On one occasion, I recognized two influential gentlemen in front of me, both long standing and often–referred–to members of the community. They were listening to the speaker, commenting back and forth and being quite critical. It seemed cruel, yet it also felt familiar–something I, and many others on the Internet, have done and continue to do nearly every day.

As members of the Fifth Estate, influencers develop new ideas and question others' opinions. Then we reinvent the ideas, publish them, bandy them about on social networks and sometimes evolve them. This development of idea memes is human nature. Consider the many conversations that occurred in fall 2010 about Mark Zuckerberg and his character as it was depicted in the Hollywood movie "The Social Network."

Influence and marketing theorist Malcolm Gladwell speculated in a fall 2010 *New Yorker* article that social networks and the influencers behind them don't really effect social change. This reflected a rigid, relevant view of influencers but perhaps was grounded in old data.[181] As a result, many Internet influencers criticized the theory, citing examples of where Gladwell was wrong.[182]

When it comes to influence, assuming right and wrong or black and white can be a dangerous game. As developers of online communities, it's easy to assume a correct approach, a finite method, a sure answer based on instincts, experiences and other community examples. As a result, one's model of influence may be grounded in the current reality.

But things change. And online they seem to change even faster. Nothing can be the same as it was.

So although you can make educated judgments and decisions based on your assumptions, and often be correct, it is important to be open to change and new realities about what influence is and how to achieve it.

Consider our theories and ongoing debates about influence. Some say popularity is influence, while others say influence is tied to how many times your comments and content are shared with others.[183] Who holds sway may change at any time, depending on community reaction to positive and negative events and input. And perhaps it depends on the person—someone can become influential by of being in the right place at the right time. Anyone's sudden rise to prominence can disrupt existing community influencer roles.

The dynamics of social network technology continue to evolve. What gives someone clout can be taken away or affected by new networks, capabilities and influences.

In 2007, bloggers were pre-eminent. By 2008, Facebook and Twitter took hold, and comments began to occur on social networks. New voices, people who for whatever reason did not blog, arose to become influential. While bloggers still hold a prominent role in social networks, popularity—measured in follower counts, retweets, links and more—became crucial (and debatable) criteria of influence.

At the time of this writing, society is in the early midst of the mobile social Internet revolution. As communicators, we are just beginning to understand how pervasive mobile Web access has become, much less how this burgeoning trend affects our community influence patterns. Empirical scientific studies have just begun.

While we try to force finite concepts onto this zeitgeist, we are at the same time evolving the way it works, changing our own information patterns as we seek to understand, evolve and grow this evergreen world. Because we are in constant flux, sedentary thought and finite peanut gallery criticisms present a real danger–the danger of being left behind.

The lesson? Remain teachable. The ability to adapt keeps us relevant.

Chapter Seven Snapshots

As social media initiatives mature and communities are built, organizations meet a new challenge: How to stay relevant. This issue is more complex than simple product marketing. With the Fifth Estate it includes a changing choice in issues, as well as in technology platforms. Further, as more members participate in your social media, the actual role of your community management changes.

Social Network Agnosticism (The Death of Facebook)

Facebook is a dominant voice in the social media world, but it, like almost every one of its predecessors, is likely to lose its place as industry leader. As technologies evolve, the community moves to new platforms, and communicators and executives need to be prepared to move with them rather than becoming overinvested in one platform.

Mobility As the Next Thing

If there is any next big thing happening in online media, it's mobility. Mobile Web use will supersede static landline use by 2014, causing a need to focus on how to make Web content more effective for mobile users.

Attitudes Toward Technology Evolution

Organizations that have been successful with their social communities over a period of years demonstrate an attitude of service. They evolve their technology platforms to serve their unique communites needs and foster more interaction. Further, they integrate themselves into larger conversations that are occurring on the Internet using social media.

Evolving Community Management

Similarly, content initiatives and community management evolve to meet the needs of the community and facilitate the end result. Sometimes this means taking the role of facilitator instead of lead voice, and even enforcing guidelines to ensure the community stays on track.

Changing Influence

A great deal of the online world revolves around influencers, but black–and–white models of influence don't accurately depict an evolving Internet. Influence can be momentary and become subject to dramatic shifts caused by technology evolution. Organizations should remain open to new influencers.

Afterword

All created things are impermanent. Strive on with diligence.
—*Guatama Buddha*

The most ruthless of political minds and the most loving of spiritual sages wrote about change. Centuries and even millennia ago, wise men like Machiavelli and Sun Tzu and the Buddha all that understood change is a fundamental reality.

Indeed, from the simple presence of Fifth Estate feedback to the evolving nature of communities and technology, change has become the unifying principle of our conversation about online communications. And that's my one desire for you, the reader, to understand that this entire online world is in a constant state of flux, and that so long as we participate in it, we will always be changing to meet the times.

Change has been hard for communicators to embrace.

Whether it was a refusal to participate in online conversations when blogs first emerged to the current painful adoption period where messages are delivered on social networks with increasing frequency, the trials and tribulations of change have been significant.

When I first began discussing the maturation of the social media technology adoption curve, colleagues began professing an opinion that the general public needs to better understand social media and that because of networked effects, social media supersedes traditional media. These voices feel that online is a mirror of our reality, only exponential, and that enough people are not participating yet. Until the public better understands and participates more, the voices of dissent feel that social media has not been adopted.

As a professional I want more voices, too; however, I disagree on one fundamental level: The Fifth Estate doesn't care about social media. They care about their lives, and information gathering and participation simply serves that, regardless of medium.

First, professional interest in how social media is used or how the communications technology is being adopted is just that—professional interest. The average consumer does not care about social media best practices, they just use it when it suits them. Just like they would a treat a movie, a book or TV program. That's not traditional media thinking, that's reality.

People don't care about communicators, tools, comment boxes, GPS check-ins or any of that junk. They don't. They care about their dinner, their children, their job security, whether or not their team won, how they can help their community.

The industries that have a vested interest–technology

and communications–in the technology's adoption do care. While one can try to differentiate new media and traditional media attitudes, it's still talking like technology and media professionals. The average consumer just isn't concerned about how relationships are being built or not being built, how revolutions are being formed or how earthquake relief is being gathered. They just do or don't participate in these things. They vote with their fingertips, either consciously or subconsciously.

Our job as professionals is to become valuable to them, to offer something of interest. Now that we have social media, we're lucky because if we're successful in at least a minimal level of engagement, we're getting feedback and can better ourselves.

Technology is not people. Technology is technology. Technology adoption is determined by percentage of use. Analyzing people's use patterns or purpose, the "proper" use of these tools, or conscious knowledge of their use of social media technology does not affect that percentage. Diffusion theory remains the same, as do the numbers. The numbers don't lie.

Ironically, my determination that the social media adoption curve was maturing was based on the more conservative of two reports on demographics as determined by age. An eMarketer study that came out at the same time demonstrated that social media technology adoption is even further along.

I have a great professional passion for social media, and I am thrilled to see other industry experts do, too. My sense about the debates about social media is that there has been an overemphasis on the tools, as well as a lot of conversation about the dramatic change they have brought to professional approaches to communications.

With social media, there's so much more that we can accomplish to better our societies, especially now that most people in America have access to these tools. I don't think social media technology adoption is the end of the road for communications. After all the widespread use of libraries in society did not end learning. On the contrary, the availability of more conversations is really just the beginning.

It's now incumbent upon us to make a compelling conversation for our stakeholders. To do that we have to change as they change and maintain a continuously relevant dialogue, regardless of medium available or tool used. We are fortunate to live in a time when this is possible.

Notes

[1] Jackie Rosseau-Anderson, "The Latest Global Social Media Trends May Surprise You." Forrester Marketing Blog, September 28, 2010 http://blogs.forrester.com/jackie_rousseau_anderson/10-09-28-latest_global_social_media_trends_may_surprise_you.

[2] Mary Madden, Older Adults and Social Media, Pew Internet, August 27, 2010 pewinternet.org/Reports/2010/Older-Adults-and-Social-Media/Report.aspx.

[3] Doriano Carter, The Future of Blogging, GigaOm, March 3, 2010, pewinternet.org/Reports/2010/Older-Adults-and-Social-Media/Report.aspx

[4] Adam Aleman, "Exposed: How Dem Party Operatives Plan on Youtubing Republicans in 2008," FlashReport, May 22, 2007 (http://www.flashreport.org/blog.php?postID=2007052203510081).

[5] Robb Tokatakiya, "The George Allen Implosion Continues," Tokatakiya, October 30, 2006 (http://tokatakiya.blogspot.com/2006/10/george-allen-implosion-continues.html).

[6] Campwood, "Fourth Estate," http://www.campwood.com/FourthEstate.htm

[7] Fourth estate, Wikipedia, http://en.wikipedia.org/wiki/Fourth_estate

[8] Valeria Maltoni, Will New Media Re-Imagine Journalism?, Conversation Agent, December 30, 2007 (http://www.conversationagent.com/2007/12/will-new-media.html).

[9] Edelman Public Relations, Edelman trustbarometer, 2010, page 6, http://www.scribd.com/full/26268655?access_key=key-1ovbgbpawooot3hnsz3u

[10] Stephen D. Cooper, "Watching the Watchdog: Bloggers as the Fifth Estate," Marquette Books, 2006.

[11] Liz Clark, "Increasingly, Fans Are Setting the Agenda in the Blogosphere," Washington Post, December 31, 2007.

[12] Susan Getgood, "More jetBlue Blues and some good advice from Strive," Marketing Roadmaps, March 4, 2007 (http://getgood.typepad.com/getgood_strategic_marketi/2007/03/more_jetblue_bl.html).

[13] We recommend starting with David Meerman Scott's New Rules of Marketing & PR. For a full list of resources see the appendices.

[14] Doc Searls, "Syndication and the Live Web Economy," Linux Journal, December 9, 2005 (http://www.linuxjournal.com/article/8731).

[15] "Web Attack," Bloomberg Businessweek, April 16, 2007, (http://www.businessweek.com/magazine/content/07_16/b4030068.htm).

[16] Fast Company, The Influencer Project (http://influenceproject.fastcompany.com/).

[17] Laura Ries, "Origin of Brands Author Laura Ries Discusses New Media," The Buzz Bin, April 23, 2007 (http://www.livingstonbuzz.com/blog/2007/04/23/origin-of-brands-author-laura-ries-discusses-new-media/).

[18] Lauren Bloom, "Social Media: Next Dotcom Bubble?," Newsweek, January 5, 2011, http://www.newsweek.com/2011/01/05/social-media-next-dot-com-bubble.html.

[19] Toby Bloomberg, original interview, June 9, 2007.

[20] Chris Anderson, "The Long Tail: Why The Future of Business Is Selling Less of More," Hyperion, 2006.

[21] "What is 80/20 rule," 80/20 Rule of Presenting Ideas, http://www.80-20presentationrule.com/whatisrule.html.

[22] Clay Shirky, "Power Laws, Weblogs and Inequality," <u>Clay Shirky's Writings About the Internet</u>, February 8, 2003 (http://www.shirky.com/writings/powerlaw_weblog.html).

[23] Isaac Pigott comment, "The Long Tail of Media Grows," GeoffLivingston.com, July 8, 2010 (http://geofflivingston.com/2010/07/08/the-long-tail-of-media-grows/comment-page-1/#comment-23309).

[24] Brian Solis, "New Communication Theory and New Roles for the New World of Marketing," BrianSolis.com, July 21, 2008 (http://www.briansolis.com/2008/07/new-communication-theory-and-new-roles/).

[25] Geoff Livingston, "Pepsi's Super Refreshing Social Play," The Buzz Bin, January 11, 2010 (http://www.livingstonbuzz.com/2010/01/11/pepsis-super-refreshing-social-play/).

[26] Toby Bloomberg, "Social Media… That's Just the Way It Is," Diva Marketing Blog, June 15, 2009 (http://bloombergmarketing.blogs.com/bloomberg_marketing/2009/06/social-media-thats-just-the-way-it-is.html).

[27] Jeremiah Owyang, "Challenges of the Social Technology Industry," Web Strategist, July 5, 2010 (http://www.web-strategist.com/blog/2010/07/05/matrix-challenges-of-the-social-technology-industry-july-2010-edition/).

[28] Jocelyn Harmon, "Slam Dunk or Snake Oil," Frogloop Blog, May 18, 2010 (http://www.frogloop.com/care2blog/2010/5/18/slam-dunk-or-snake-oil-everyone-wants-to-raise-money-with-so.html).

[29] Joseph Jaffe, "The Chase," Jaffe Juice, May 5, 2010 (http://www.jaffejuice.com/2010/05/jjtv-96-the-chase.html).

[30] Joe Wikert, "Wikinomics," 2020: Joe Wikert's Publishing Blog, Jan. 6, 2007 (http://jwikert.typepad.com/the_average_joe/2007/01/wikinomics_by_d.html).

[31] Isaac Pigott, "Social Media Is Organic," Now Is Gone, Nov. 27, 2007 (http://nowisgone.com/2007/11/27/social-media-is-organic/).

[32] Leroy Stick – the man behind @BPGobalPR, Street Giant, June 2 2010, http://streetgiant.com/2010/06/02/leroy-stick-the-man-behind-bpglobalpr/.

[33] Wendy Piersall, "10 Social Media Blunders That Can Destroy Your Brand," Sparkplug CEO, April 24, 2008 (http://www.sparkplugging.com/sparkplug-ceo/10-social-media-blunders-that-can-destroy-your-brand/).

[34] Manish Mehta, Keynote Speech, NewComm Forum, April 23, 2010.

[35] Zach Hofer-Shall, "The Forrester Wave: Listening Platforms Q3 2010," Forrester, July 2010.

[36] Allyson Kapin, "Top Five Tools for Listening on the Social Web," Frogloop Blog, July 5, 2010 (http://www.frogloop.com/care2blog/2010/7/5/top-five-tools-for-listening-on-the-social-web.html).

[37] Shel Israel, "JetBlue: How Do You Feel About Them Now," Global Neighbourhoods April 13, 2007 (http://redcouch.typepad.com/weblog/2007/04/jet_blue_how_do.html)

[38] Gary Kelly, "To Assign or Not to Assign," Nuts About Southwest, Sept. 19, 2007 (http://www.blogsouthwest.com/blog/to-assign-or-not-assign-that-question).

[39] Jay Rosen "The People Formerly Known as the Audience," Press Think, June 27, 2006 (http://journalism.nyu.edu/pubzone/weblogs/pressthink/2006/06/27/ppl_frmr.html).

[40] Marshall Kirkpatrick, "Guide to Online Community Management," ReadWriteWeb, May 14, 2008 (http://www.readwriteweb.com/archives/introducing_the_readwriteweb_guide_to_online_commu.php).

[41] Michael A. Stelzner, The Dark Side of Blogging: Warnings From Leading Bloggers, The Marketing Profs (http://www.marketingprofs.com/7/dark-side-blogging-warning-leading-bloggers-stelzner.asp).

[42] Edelman, 2010 Trust Barometer Executive Summary, Page 3 (http://www.edelman.com/trust/2010/).

[43] Rohit Bhargava, Personality Not Included, McGraw-Hill, 2008.

[44] Robert Scoble and Shel Israel, Naked Conversations, Wiley, 2006.

[45] David Meerman Scott, "Personal Brands vs. corporate brands: Who are the real superstars?" WebInkNow, Aug. 24, 2009 (http://www.webinknow.com/2009/08/personal-brands-vs-corporate-brands-who-are-the-real-superstars.html).

[46] Geoff Livingston, "I Don't Care About Your Personal Brand," The Buzz Bin, Nov. 6, 2008 (http://www.livingstonbuzz.com/2008/11/06/i-dont-care-about-your-personal-brand/).

[47] Geoff Livingston, "Brand and Reputation Are Not Synonymous," The Buzz Bin, July 13, 2009 (http://www.livingstonbuzz.com/2009/07/13/brand-and-reputation-are-not-synonymous/).

[48] James Chartrand, "Are You In Personal Branding Prison?" CopyBlogger, May 8, 2008 (http://www.copyblogger.com/personal-branding-prison/).

[49] Michael Donnell Brown, "The Dangers of Personal Brand Overpromotion," eZine Articles, 2010 (http://ezinearticles.com/?The-Dangers-of-Personal-Brand-Overpromotion&id=4212504).

[50] James Chartrand, "The Dangers of Personal Branding," Freelance Switch, Feb. 21, 2010 (http://freelanceswitch.com/the-business-of-freelancing/the-dangers-of-personal-branding/).

[51] Joel Keller, "Donald Trump's Ego is The Celebrity Apprentice's Biggest Problem," TV Squad, March 15, 2010 (http://www.tvsquad.com/2010/03/15/donald-trumps-ego-is-the-celebrity-apprentices-biggest-probl/).

52 MDB, "About Authentic Personal Branding," Miboso, http://authenticpersonalbranding.com/about/.

53 Geoff Livingston, "Team Social Media," The Buzz Bin, Feb. 3, 2009 (http://www.livingstonbuzz.com/2009/02/03/team-social-media/).

54 Geoff Livingston, Top Five Organizational Silos, The Buzz Bin, August, 31, 2009 (http://www.livingstonbuzz.com/2009/08/31/five-top-organizational-silos/)

55 The United States Air Force, New Media and the Air Force, April 6, 2009, page 5 *(www.af.mil/shared/***media***/document/AFD-090406-036.pdf).*

56 Greg Verdino, MicroMarketing, 2010: McGraw Hill, Kindle location 1172.

57 Heidi Sullivan, 5 Best Practices for Creating a Social Media Policy, CisionBlog, May 26, 2009 (http://blog.us.cision.com/2009/05/5-best-practices-for-creating-a-corporate-social-media-policy/).

58 Isaac Pigott, The Future of Journalism Part II, Occam's Razr, April 6, 2010 (http://occamsrazr.com/2010/04/06/the-future-of-journalism-part-two/).

59 Alexander Howard, Emergency Social Data Summit, Huffington Post, August 16, 2010 (http://www.huffingtonpost.com/alexander-howard/emergency-social-data-sum_b_682292.html).

60 Beth Kanter and Allison Fine, Networked Nonprofit, New York: Jossey Bass, 2010.

61 Jackie Huba, Loyalty Lessons from Lady Gaga, Church of the Customer, February 23, 2010, http://www.churchofcustomer.com/2010/02/loyalty-lessons-from-lady-gaga.html.

62 Josh Bernoff, People Don't Trust Company Blogs, Empowered Blog, December 9, 2008 (http://forrester.typepad.com/groundswell/2008/12/people-dont-tru.html)

63 eMarketer, "Who Finds Twittter More Effective – Advertisers or Consumers?," eMarketer, August 4, 2009 (http://www.emarketer.com/Article.aspx?R=1007208).

[64] Allison Fine, Creating a Social Culture, A Fine Blog, September 4, 2009 (http://afine2.wordpress.com/2009/09/03/creating-a-social-culture/).

[65] Mark Story, Reality Check, the intersection of online and offline, December 1, 2008 (http://www.intersectionofonlineandoffline.com/reality-check-there-will-be-no-wiki-white-house-dan/).

[66] Geoff Livingston, Moving from Silos to Hives, The Buzz Bin, April 6, 2009 (http://www.livingstonbuzz.com/2009/04/06/moving-from-siloes-to-hives/).

[67] Kami Huyse, Engaging External Audiences with Internal Culture, Communication Overtones, September 4, 2009 (http://overtonecomm.blogspot.com/2009/09/inside-out-engaging-external-audiences.html)

[68] Charlene Li, "Announcing My Next Book," The Altimeter, August 18, 2009 (http://www.altimetergroup.com/2009/08/announcing-my-next-book.html).

[69] Anonymous, "Contemplating the Soft Infrastructure of Social Media," HeavySet, March 17, 2009 (http://www.hvyset.com/2009/03/contemplating-the-soft-infrastructure-of-social-media/).

[70] Kevin Houchin, Play Nice, Houchin & Associates, December 8, 2008 (http://houchinlaw.com/2008/12/08/play-nice-legal-issues-social-media/).

[71] Robin Broitman, Social Media Case Studies Superlist, Interactive Insights Group, December 3, 2008 (http://www.interactiveinsightsgroup.com/blog1/social-media-examples-superlist-17-lists-and-tons-of-examples/).

[72] Jason Falls, "Four Styles of Marketing on Twitter," Social Media Explorer, January 18, 2010 (http://www.socialmediaexplorer.com/2010/01/18/four-styles-of-marketing-on-twitter/).

[73] Jeremiah Owyang, The 8 Success Criteria for Facebook Page Marketing, The Altimeter, July 28, 2010 (http://www.altimetergroup.com/2010/07/altimeter-report-the-8-success-criteria-for-facebook-page-marketing.html).

[74] "Beehive," Wikipedia, last modified on August 30, 2010 (http://en.wikipedia.org/wiki/Beehive).

[75] Alex Penton, Honest Signals, Boston, MA: MIT Press (1st edition), 2008.

[76] Chris Boudreaux, Policy Database, Social Media Governance, 2010 (http://socialmediagovernance.com/policies.php).

[77] Wendy Harman, Social Media Strategy Handbook, The American Red Cross, July 16, 2009 (http://sites.google.com/site/wharman/social-media-strategy-handbook).

[78] Shel Holtz, If You're Not Participating, You're Invisible, a shel of my former self, August 24, 2010 (http://blog.holtz.com/index.php/weblog/if_youre_not_participating_youre_invisible/).

[79] Pete Caputa, Internet Marketers are from Mars. Traditional Marketers are from Venus, HubSpot Blog, February 10, 2009, (http://blog.hubspot.com/blog/tabid/6307/bid/4556/Internet-Marketers-are-from-Mars-Traditional-Marketers-are-from-Venus.aspx).

[80] eMarketer, The State of Social Marketing Integration, eMarketer, March 19, 2010 (http://www.emarketer.com/Article.aspx?R=1007579).

[81] Tim Leberecht, The Permanent Crisis of Marketing, Frog Design Mind, February 14, 2009 (http://designmind.frogdesign.com/blog/the-new-permanent-crisis-of-marketing.html).

[82] Al Ries and Jack Trout, Positioning, 3rd Edition, McGraw Hill, New York, 2000.

[83] Cindy King, Definition of a Brand, Cindy King, January 9, 2009, (http://cindyking.biz/branding-and-building-an-international-business/).

[84] Sun Tzu, The Art of War, Think Exist, 500 BC, http://thinkexist.com/quotation/the_art_of_war_teaches_us_to_rely_not_on_the/149712.html.

[85] Dan Heath, keynote speech, Consumer Electronics Association annual meeting, October 18, 2007.

[86] Kami Watson Huyse, original interview, June 8, 2007.

[87] Mario Sundar, "Face Book Polls: Market Research Meets Social Networks," Marketing Nirvana, June 3, 2007 (http://mariosundar.wordpress.com/2007/06/03/facebook-polls-market-research-meets-social-networks/).

[88] Gaspedal, "social media case study from Bert Dumars of Newell Rubbermaid," Business Blogging Blog, January 27, 2010, (http://www.socialmedia.org/blog/social-media-case-study-from-bert-dumars-of-newell-rubbermaid/).

[89] Susan Getgood, "BlogHer Marketing Lessons Part 2: Influencer Relations and #gapmagic," Marketing Roadmaps, August 13, 2010, (http://getgood.com/roadmaps/2010/08/13/blogher-marketing-lessons-part-2-influencer-relations-and-gapmagic/).

[90] Todd Defren, "Shiny Object Syndrome," PR Squared, September 1, 2005, (http://www.pr-squared.com/2005/09/shiny_object_syndrome.html).

[91] Jeremiah Owyang, "Stop Fondling the Hammer, and Focus on the House," Web Strategist, January 17, 2008, (http://www.web-strategist.com/blog/2008/01/17/stop-focusing-on-the-hammer-and-think-about-the-house/).

[92] Todd Defren, "Shiny Object Syndrome," PR Squared, September 1, 2005, (http://www.pr-squared.com/2005/09/shin

[93] Beth Kanter, "Getting Beyond Shiny Object Syndrome," Beth's Blog, July 26, 2008, (http://beth.typepad.com/beths_blog/2008/07/nptech-summary.html).

[94] Chris Heuer, "Participation is Marketing," The Future of Communities, March 12, 2007, (http://www.futureofcommunities.com/2007/03/12/participation-is-marketing/).

[95] Ibid.

[96] Ibid.

[97] Brian Solis, Humanizing Social Networks, BrianSolis.com, March 11, 2009, (http://www.briansolis.com/2009/03/humanizing-social-networks-revealing/).

[98] David Meerman Scott, The New Rules of Marketing & PR, John Wiley & Sons, Inc. (Hoboken, New Jersey: 2007), p. 38.

[99] Janna Anderson, Lee Ranie, "The Future of Social Relations," Pew Internet, July 2, 2010 (http://www.pewinternet.org/Reports/2010/The-future-of-social-relations/Overview.aspx).

[100] Clive Thompson, "Is the Tipping Point Toast?," Fast Company, February 1, 2008 (http://www.fastcompany.com/magazine/122/is-the-tipping-point-toast.html?page=0%2C1).

[101] Wikipedia, "Dunbar's Number," Wikipedia, August 30, 2010 (http://en.wikipedia.org/wiki/Dunbar%27s_number).

[102] David Sifry, "State of the Blogosphere, February 2006, Part II," Sifrey's Alerts, February 13, 2006 (http://www.sifry.com/alerts/archives/000420.html).

[103] Rory Cellan-Jones, "Twitter and the China Earthquake," BBC News dot.life, May 12, 2008 (http://www.bbc.co.uk/blogs/technology/2008/05/twitter_and_the_china_earthqua.html).

[104] Allyson Kapin, "Crowdsourcing and Community Building, the Big Buzz at SxSW 2010," FrogLoop, March 18, 2010 (http://www.frogloop.com/care2blog/2010/3/18/crowdsourcing-and-community-building-the-big-buzz-at-sxsw.html).

[105] Geoff Livingston, "Idiots and Gossip," The Buzz Bin, January 4, 2009 http://www.livingstonbuzz.com/2009/01/04/idiots-and-gossip-plus-other-tales-from-the-sociometer/).

[106] Guido Juiret, "Inside Cisco's Search for the Next Big Idea," Harvard Business Review, September 2009, (http://hbr.org/2009/09/inside-ciscos-search-for-the-next-big-idea/ar/1).

[107] Marshall Kirkpatrick, Introducing the ReadWriteWeb Guide to Community Management, ReadWriteWeb, May 14, 2009 (http://www.readwriteweb.com/archives/introducing_the_readwriteweb_guide_to_online_commu.php).

[108] David Talbot, "How Obama Really Did It," MIT Technology Review, September/October 2008 (http://www.technologyreview.com/

Infotech/21222/page2/).

[109] Isaac Pigott, "Social Media Is Organic," Now Is Gone blog, Nov. 27, 2007 http://nowisgone.com/2007/11/27/social-media-is-organic/.

[110] Augie Ray, "The Implications of Consumers Spending Time with Facebook than Google," Sept. 10, 2010, http://blogs.forrester.com/augie_ray/10-09-10-implications_consumers_spending_more_time_facebook_google.

[111] Geoff Livingston, "5 Social Media Lessons from the Haiti Earthquake Relief Effort," Mashable, Jan. 20, 2010, http://mashable.com/2010/01/20/social-media-lessons-haiti/.

[112] John Bell, "How to Reproduce the Old Spice Video Phenomena," Digital Influence Mapping Project, July 19, 2010, http://johnbell.typepad.com/weblog/2010/07/how-to-reproduce-the-old-spice-video-phenomena.html.

[113] Toby Bloomberg, Social Media… That's Just the Way It Is, Diva Marketing Blog, June 15, 2009, http://bloombergmarketing.blogs.com/bloomberg_marketing/2009/06/social-media-thats-just-the-way-it-is.html.

[114] David Henderson, Unique Positioning in One Sentence, David E. Henderson, April 16, 2009, http://www.davidhenderson.com/2009/04/16/unique-positioning-in-a-sentence/.

[115] Dale Carnegie, "How to Win Friends & Influence People," New York: Pocket Edition, June 15, 2009.

[116] Meg Keaney and Geoff Livingston, Social Network Participation, Slideshare, May 14, 2009, http://www.slideshare.net/geoliv/social-network-participation.

[117] Shonali Burke, " Samuel Gordon Jewlers: A Small Business That Gets Social Media," BNET, September 28, 2010, http://www.bnet.com/blog/smb/samuel-gordon-jewelers-a-small-business-that-gets-social-media/2274?tag=mantle_skin;content.

[118] Dan Gordon, email interview conducted on October 13, 2010.

[119] Shonali Burke, " Samuel Gordon Jewlers: A Small Business That Gets Social Media," BNET, September 28, 2010, http://www.bnet.com/blog/smb/samuel-gordon-jewelers-a-small-business-that-gets-social-media/2274?tag=mantle_skin;content.

[120] Sonali Burke, email interview conducted on October 14, 2010

[121] Gordon, Ibid.

[122] Amy Stodgehill, "Got an Idea for a Green Ad Campaign," Green Options, March 3, 2007, http://www.greenoptions.com/blog/2007/03/03/got_an_idea_for_a_green_ad_campaign_send_it_to_yahoo.

[123] Mary Madden, "Older Adults and Social Media," Pew Internet, Aug. 27, 2010, http://www.pewinternet.org/Reports/2010/Older-Adults-and-Social-Media.aspx.

[124] Susan Getgood, original interview, Aug. 9, 2010.

[125] Why Most Online Communities Fail, WSJ Blog: Digits, July 16, 2008, http://blogs.wsj.com/biztech/2008/07/16/why-most-online-communities-fail/

[126] Mike Volpe, State of the Twittersphere Q4 2008, Hubspot Blog, Dec. 22, 2008, http://blog.hubspot.com/blog/tabid/6307/bid/4439/State-of-the-Twittersphere-Q4-2008-Report.aspx.

[127] Andrew Redfern, Facebook Opens Policy Process to the Masses, Redfern, Feb. 27, 2009, http://www.hitsearchlimited.com/news/9992054/.

[128] Geoff Livingston, Nuts About Southwest Demonstrates True Social Interaction, The Buzz Bin, May 8, 2007, http://www.livingstonbuzz.com/2007/05/08/nuts-about-southwest-demonstrates-true-social-interaction/.

[129] Lee Odden, Reputation Management for Affiliate Marketing, Top Rank Blog, Jan. 21, 2009, http://www.toprankblog.com/2009/01/reputation-management-for-affiliate-marketing/.

[130] Elliot Back, Exploding Dell Laptop Battery, Elliot C. Back: Internet Technology, Aug. 20, 2006, http://elliottback.com/wp/exploding-dell-

laptop-battery-bonanza/.

[131] Mireya Navarro, Pout and Shout, New York Times, Dec. 2, 2007, http://www.nytimes.com/2007/12/02/fashion/02fans.html?_r=3&oref=slogin.

[132] Eric Eggertson, Fast Action In a Crisis Can Get Your Message Heard, Every Joe.com, April 18, 2007, http://everyjoe.com/work/fast-action-in-a-crisis-can-get-your-message-heard-168/?utm_source=everyjoe&utm_medium=web&utm_campaign=b5hubs_migration

[133] Valeria Maltoni, Restoring the Faith in Popcorn, Conversation Agent, Sept. 14, 2007, http://www.conversationagent.com/2007/09/restoring-the-f.html.

[134] Susan Getgood, Feeding the Trolls, Marketing Roadmaps, Oct. 12, 2007, http://getgood.typepad.com/getgood_strategic_marketi/2007/10/feeding-the-tro.html.

[135] "Cluetrain Manifesto" (Copyright 2000 Reed Business Information Inc.), by Rick Levine, Christopher Locke, Doc Searls, David Weinberger, and Jake McKee

[136] Social Marketing Analytics by Jeremiah Owyang, of the Altimeter Group, John Lovett and Eric Peterson (ex-Jupiter analyst) both of the Web Analytics Demystified http://www.slideshare.net/jeremiah_owyang/altimeter-report-social-marketing-analytics

[137] Website Strategy by Jeremiah Owyang, "Altimeter Report: Social Marketing Analytics (Altimeter Group & Web Analytics Demystified), http://www.web-strategist.com/blog/2010/04/22/altimeter-report-social-marketing-analytics-with-web-analytics-demystified/

[138] SMART criteria mnemonic used in project management http://en.wikipedia.org/wiki/SMART_criteria

[139] Doran, George T. "There's a S.M.A.R.T. way to write management's goals and objectives." Management Review, Nov 1981, Volume 70 Issue 11.

[140] Key Performance Indicators (KPI), "How an organization defines and measures progress toward its goals," By F. John Reh, About.com Guide http://management.about.com/cs/generalmanagement/a/

keyperfindic.htm

141 Greenopolis, http://greenopolis.com/

142 California surfer receives whale of an escort during marathon paddle, *Grind TV in Association with Yahoo Sports,*

http://www.grindtv.com/outdoor/blog/16812/california+surfer+receives+whale+of+an+escort+during+marathon+paddle/

143 This result taken from free eGuide Cause Marketing Through Social Media: 5 Steps to Successful Campaigns, by Kate Olson and Geoff Livingston. Download at http://www1.networkforgood.org/causemarketing

144 Case study based on an interview conducted by Kami Watson Huyse with Connie Chan, manager, Yahoo! for Good, Sept. 29, 2010.

145 *Measuring Public Relationships, The Data-Driven Communicator's Guide to Success* by Katie Delahayne Paine, 228 pages, paperback. ISBN 978-0-9789899-0-3. http://kdpaine.blogs.com/bookblog/2007/12/kdpaine-partner.html

146 The New York Times, The Value of a Facebook Friend? About 37 Cents, by Jenna Wortham, January 9, 2009, http://bits.blogs.nytimes.com/2009/01/09/are-facebook-friends-worth-their-weight-in-beef/

147 Katie Paine's Dirty Dozen Public Relations Measurement Mistakes, September 10, 2010, http://kdpaine.blogs.com/themeasurementstandard/2010/09/katie-paines-dirty-dozen-public-relations-measurement-mistakes.html

148 Northwestern University Press Release (see press releases are not dead), http://www.eecs.northwestern.edu/the-news/363-website-ranks-most-influential-tweeters.html

149 Pulse of Tweeters tool, http://www.pulseofthetweeters.com/

150 "What Is The Value Of A Facebook Fan? Zero!" Forrester Blog, by Augie Raye, senior analyst of Social Computing, Forrester Research, July 8, 2010

http://blogs.forrester.com/augie_ray/10-07-08-what_value_facebook_

fan_zero?utm_source=feedburner&utm_medium=feed&utm_campaig
n=Feed:+ForresterMarketing+(The+Forrester+Blog+For+Interactive+
Marketing+Professionals)

[151] Time Flies: Looking Back at a Year of Using Social Media, Dr. http://
www2.mdanderson.org/cancerwise/2010/08/looking-back-at-a-year-of-
using-social-media.html

[152] Cancerwise Blog, MD Anderson, http://www2.mdanderson.org/
cancerwise/

[153] Guidelines for Measuring the Effectiveness of PR Programs and
Activities, By Dr. Walter K. Lindenmann, Copyright 1997, 2003 Institute
for Public Relations, www.instituteforpr.org

[154] Engagementdb, Altimeter and Wetpaint, 2009 http://engagementdb.
com/

[155] Basics of Social Media ROI, Olivier Blanchard, http://www.
slideshare.net/thebrandbuilder/olivier-blanchard-basics-of-
social-media-roi

[156] Falls, Jason . "Why You Shouldn't Trust Automated Sentiment
Scoring." Social Media Explorer. 26 Apr. 2010. http://www.
socialmediaexplorer.com/social-media-monitoring/trusting-
automated-sentiment-scoring/.

[157] Kaushik, Avinash, "Web Analytics 2.0: The Art of Online
Accountability & Science of Customer Centricity," Wiley Publishing,
Inc., 2010.

[158] "Guidelines for Measuring Relationships in Public Relations," Linda
Childers Hon and James E. Grunig Institute for Public Relations,
http://www.instituteforpr.org/research_single/guidelines_measuring_
relationships/

[159] Communication Overtones, "How To: The Secrets for Gaming
Twitter Are Free, and Why It Doesn't Matter Anyway," by Kami Huyse,
March 11, 2009, http://overtonecomm.blogspot.com/2009/03/how-to-
secrets-for-gaming-twitter-are.html

[160] Amnesia Blog, "How to spot a Twitter User with a 'Fake' follower

count", by Iain McDonald, March 22nd, 2009, http://amnesiablog. wordpress.com/2009/03/22/how-to-spot-a-twitter-user-with-a-fake-follower-count/

[161] Dashes: A Blog About Making Culture, "Nobody Has a Million Twitter Followers," by Anil Dash, January 5, 2010, http://dashes.com/anil/2010/01/nobody-has-a-million-twitter-followers.html

[163] GigaOm, "The Value of Twitter Followers: Quality Over Quantity, By Aliza Sherman July 2, 2009, http://gigaom.com/collaboration/the-value-of-twitter-followers-quality-over-quantity/

[163] Google Analytics URL Builder, http://www.google.com/support/analytics/bin/answer.py?hl=en&answer=55518

[164] Randy Paynter, "The Desert of Community Building (Comment)," Geoff Livingston's blog, September 12, 2010, http://geofflivingston.com/2010/09/12/the-desert-of-community-building/.

[165] John Bell, How to Reproduce the Old Spice Video Phenomena, Digital Influence Mapping Project, July 19, 2010, http://johnbell.typepad.com/weblog/2010/07/how-to-reproduce-the-old-spice-video-phenomena.html.

[166] Geoff Livingston, "Think Liquid," Now Is Gone blog, September 1, 2007, http://nowisgone.com/2007/09/01/think-liquid/.

[167] Charlene Li and Josh Bernoff, Groundswell, Harvard University Business Press, Boston, MA: 2008.

[168] National Center for Charitable Statistics, Number of nonprofits in the U.S. (1998-2008), http://nccsdataweb.urban.org/PubApps/profile1.php.

[169] National Conference on Citizenship, Civic Life in America, Fact Sheet, September, 2010.

[170] Levi Sumagaysay, "While You're at It, Facebook...," Good Morning Silicon Valley, August 26, 2010, http://blogs.siliconvalley.com/gmsv/2010/08/while-youre-at-it-facebook-weve-noticed-that-pesky-amazon-uses-book-a-lot-too.html.

[171] Ryan Singel, Facebook's Mark Zuckerberg Becomes Poster Childe for

New Privacy Settings, Epicenter, December 11, 2009, http://www.wired.com/epicenter/2009/12/zuckerberg-facebook-privacy/.

[172] Aaron Smith, Mobile Access 2010, Pew Internet, July 7, 2010, http://www.wired.com/epicenter/2009/12/zuckerberg-facebook-privacy/.

[173] Catharine Smith, "Android Beats iPhone," Huffington Post, October 5, 2010, http://www.huffingtonpost.com/2010/10/05/nielsen-android-most-popular_n_751155.html

[174] Matthew Ingram, Mobile Internet Will Soon Overtake Fixed Internet, Gigaom, April 12, 2010, http://gigaom.com/2010/04/12/mary-meeker-mobile-internet-will-soon-overtake-fixed-internet/

[175] Michael Schneider and Anne Mai Bertelsen, Beyond Foursquare, Harvard Business Review Blogs, October 4, 2010, http://blogs.hbr.org/cs/2010/10/beyond_foursquare_the_next_gen.html.

[176] Jaya Saxena, Map Track's City's Activity through Foursquare, August 21, 2010, The Gothamist, http://gothamist.com/2010/08/21/map_tracks_citys_social_activity_th.php.

[177] Interviews were conducted with Randy Paynter, Co-Founder, Care2; Peggy Duvette, Executive Director, Wiser Earth; Patrick Crane, Vice President of Marketing, LinkedIn; Richard Binhammer, Digital Media, Digital Corporate Communications, Dell; and Carie Lewis, Director of Emerging Media, Humane Society of America between September 28 and October 8, 2010.

[178] Geoff Livingston, "4 Real Challenges to Crowdsourcing Social Good," Mashable, October 12, 2010, http://mashable.com/2010/10/12/social-good-crowdsourcing/.

[179] Ibid.

[180] Scott Harrison, How Birthdays are Changing are the World, Huffington Post, October 4, 2010, http://www.huffingtonpost.com/scott-harrison/how-birthdays-are-changin_b_748737.html

[181] Malcolm Gladwell, Small Change, The New Yorker, October 4, 2010, http://www.newyorker.com/reporting/2010/10/04/101004fa_fact_gladwell.

[182] Anil Dash, Make the Revolution, Anil Dash, September 28, 2010, http://dashes.com/anil/2010/09/when-the-revolution-comes-they-wont-recognize-it.html

[183] Brian Solis, Exploring and Defining Influence, Brian Solis, September 29, 2010, http://www.briansolis.com/2010/09/exploring-and-defining-influence-a-new-study/